Second Workshop on NLP Applications to Field Linguistics (Field Matters 2023)

Dubrovnik, Croatia
6 May 2023

ISBN: 978-1-7138-9050-8

Printed from e-media with permission by:

Curran Associates, Inc.
57 Morehouse Lane
Red Hook, NY 12571

Some format issues inherent in the e-media version may also appear in this print version.

Printed with permission by Curran Associates, Inc. (2024)

For permission requests, please contact the Association for Computational Linguistics at the address below.

Association for Computational Linguistics
209 N. Eighth Street
Stroudsburg, Pennsylvania 18360

Phone: 1-570-476-8006
Fax: 1-570-476-0860

acl@aclweb.org

Additional copies of this publication are available from:

Curran Associates, Inc.
57 Morehouse Lane
Red Hook, NY 12571 USA
Phone: 845-758-0400
Fax: 845-758-2633
Email: curran@proceedings.com
Web: www.proceedings.com

FieldMatters 2023

The Second Workshop on NLP Applications to Field Linguistics (Field Matters)

Proceedings of the Workshop

May 6, 2023

Preface by the General Chair

Field Matters is a workshop focused on various applications of NLP methods to field linguistics and analysis of field data with the help of computational linguistics.
On the one hand, field linguists document language data, but the fieldwork involves tons of manual annotation or analysis, which might be significantly sped up with computational instruments. On the other hand, NLP research brought methods for different tasks that show significant performance in high-resource languages, allowing to automate various routine tasks. The future development of NLP methods could gain from the language diversity of under-resourced languages. Field Matters is aimed to combine linguistic fieldwork and NLP methods. Our workshop is hosted by the 17th Conference of the European Chapter of the Association for Computational Linguistics (EACL 2023).
To provide the comprehensive diverse expertise in a multidisciplinary setting, for the second time we invite linguists and NLP researchers worldwide to our program committee. After the hard process of reviewing all submissions, the program committee chose nine papers for a poster or oral presentation at the workshop. Accepted papers illustrate the main idea of our workshop: how field linguistics may benefit from using contemporary methods of computational analysis and how the NLP community may evolve its methods with the help of underresourced languages.
More specifically, chosen papers cover the following topics:

- use of ASR into the field linguistic pipeline
- use of computational methods to provide deterministic grounding for the language documentation insights
- incorporating linguistic knowledge to the neural language processing algorithms despite the low-resourced setting
- using Information Extraction algorithms to support the language documentation
- building tools for native speakers community

Following the key insight of the FM2022, in some studies, the collaborative nature of the process has taken its place, making the results useful for both researchers and native speakers.
Notably, the recently popularized Limitations section has proven itself useful. Several papers contain meaningful insights into the state of the field or language nuanced details worth attention themselves. Given 24 submissions in total (including 3 papers submitted through the ACL Findings program), the acceptance rate is $11/24$, with 4 papers selected for oral presentation.
We are incredibly grateful to the Field Matters program committee, who worked on peer review to give meaningful comments for each submission and made this workshop possible. We want to thank the invited speakers, Lane Swartz and Emmanuel Schang, for contributing to the program. We would also like to mention all the authors who submitted their papers to our workshop, and we hope to continue to serve as a link between NLP specialists and field linguists.

Organizing Committee

General Chairs

Oleg Serikov, Independent Researcher
Ekaterina Voloshina, Independent Researcher
Anna Postnikova, Independent Researcher
Elena Klyachko, Independent Researcher
Ekaterina Vylomova, University of Melbourne
Tatiana Shavrina, Independent Researcher
Eric Le Ferrand, Universite Grenoble Alpes, Universite d'Orleans
Valentin Malykh, Huawei
Francis Tyers, Indiana University, HSE University
Timofey Arkhangelskiy, University of Hamburg
Vladislav Mikhailov, Independent Researcher

Program Committee

Chairs

Elena Klyachko, HSE, Institute of Linguistics RAS
Oleg Serikov, DeepPavlov, AIR Institute, HSE University
Ekaterina Voloshina, AIRI

Program Committee

Dmitry Abulkhanov, Huawei Noah's Ark
Alexandre Arkhipov, Universität Hamburg
Harald Hammarström, Uppsala University
Ezequiel Koile, Max Planck Institute for Evolutionary Anthropology
Éric Le Ferrand, Université d'Orléans
Zoey Liu, Department of Linguistics, University of Florida
Valentin Malykh, Huawei Noah's Ark Lab / Kazan Federal University
Tessa Masis, University of Massachusetts Amherst
Vladislav Mikhailov, HSE University
Saliha Muradoglu, The Australian National University
Vitaly Protasov, AIRI
Emily Prud'hommeaux, Boston College
Tatiana Shavrina, AIRI
He Zhou, Indiana University
Nadezhda Zueva, VK

Table of Contents

Program

Friday, May 5, 2023

09:00 - 10:30 *Invited talk. Lane Schwartz.*

11:15 - 12:45 *Invited talk. Emmanuel Schang.*

12:45 - 14:15 *lunch break*

14:15 - 15:45 *Presentations*

Speech Database (Speech-DB) – An on-line platform for storing, validating, searching, and recording spoken language data
Jolene Poulin, Daniel Dacanay and Antti Arppe

Improving Low-resource RRG Parsing with Structured Gloss Embeddings
Roland Eibers, Kilian Evang and Laura Kallmeyer

A Quest for Paradigm Coverage: The Story of Nen
Saliha Muradoglu, Hanna Suominen and Nicholas Evans

Unsupervised part-of-speech induction for language description: Modeling documentation materials in Kolyma Yukaghir
Albert Ventayol-boada, Nathan Roll and Simon Todd

15:45 - 16:30 *Coffee Break*

16:30 - 18:00 *Presentations*

Automated speech recognition of Indonesian-English language lessons on YouTube using transfer learning
Zara Maxwelll-smith and Ben Foley

Application of Speech Processes for the Documentation of Kréyòl Gwadloupéyen
Éric Le Ferrand, Fabiola Henri, Benjamin Lecouteux and Emmanuel Schang

ASR pipeline for low-resourced languages: A case study on Pomak
Chara Tsoukala, Kosmas Kritsis, Ioannis Douros, Athanasios Katsamanis, Nikolaos Kokkas, Vasileios Arampatzakis, Vasileios Sevetlidis, Stella Markantonatou and George Pavlidis

Friday, May 5, 2023 (continued)

Automated speech recognition of Indonesian-English language lessons on YouTube using transfer learning

Zara Maxwell-Smith
The Australian National University
Zara.Maxwell-Smith@anu.edu.au

Ben Foley
The University of Queensland
b.foley@uq.edu.au

Abstract

Experiments to fine-tune large multilingual models with limited data from a specific domain or setting has potential to improve automatic speech recognition (ASR) outcomes. This paper reports on the use of the Elpis ASR pipeline to fine-tune two pre-trained base models, Wav2Vec2-XLSR-53 and Wav2Vec2-Large-XLSR-Indonesian, with various mixes of data from 3 YouTube channels teaching Indonesian with English as the language of instruction. We discuss our results inferring new lesson audio (22-46% word error rate) in the context of speeding data collection in diverse and specialised settings. This study is an example of how ASR can be used to accelerate natural language research, expanding ethically sourced data in low-resource settings.

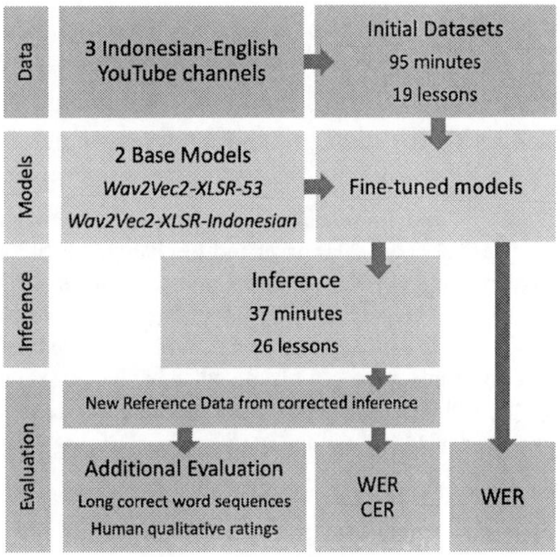

Figure 1: Study Design. See Section 2 for a detailed description of data used to fine-tune and evaluate models.

1 Introduction

Accent, speaker-class characteristics, and the use of dialects are among many factors impacting automatic speech recognition (ASR) performance (Jurafsky and Martin, 2023). The dominance of 'high-resource' languages in natural language processing (NLP) and impact of market forces have produced strong outcomes for some applications of ASR when dialects, accented speech or particular speaker populations are excluded (Faisal et al., 2021; Koenecke et al., 2020; Bishop, 2022). However, many human speech scenarios, especially outside monolingual English contexts, require technologies more robust to language mixing and situated language usage — as well as performance measures of these technologies that prioritise the needs of users (Birhane et al., 2022).

This study worked with data from a non-standard context, that is, data from three YouTube channels teaching Indonesian with English as the language of instruction. It records the teaching practice of three teachers who: 1) explore a broad definition of 'Indonesian language', 2) demonstrate various linguistic behaviours associated with teaching (e.g., hyper-articulation and repetition), 3) would typically be described as 'accented' in either one or both languages, and 4) recorded their speech amidst background noise, adding music and sound effects. We hypothesised that repetition and simplifications in 'teacher-talk' intended to create comprehensible input for students (Krashen, 1981), and the use of transfer learning, could balance the many challenging characteristics in the data and allow ASR to create useful transcriptions for editing and analysis.

In recent years, transfer learning approaches have achieved state-of-the-art ASR performance on benchmark tasks with small quantities of data (Church et al., 2021). These approaches fine-tune a base model previously trained on a large dataset. Some pretrained models have been made publicly available, allowing more people to take advantage of their performance, and their advantages to be shared more equitably (Scao et al., 2022).

Proceedings of the Second Workshop on NLP Applications to Field Linguistics, pages 1–16
May 6, 2023 ©2023 Association for Computational Linguistics

Data sample 1 - Participant Eiphel Mercedec

1.1	We prefer [to] call it [some people, in certain circumstances] **kak.** *(shortened version of Indonesian 'kakak' – older sibling)*
1.2	Some people use **mbak** as an older sister [to refer to an older sister]. *(Javanese – older sister)*
1.3	Or **mas** as [for] an older brother. *(Javanese- older brother)*
1.4	This is a Javanese version [of this set of address terms].
1.5	If you're Indonesia[n] you also experience [being called] **mbak** which is the same as *(Javanese – older sister)* older sister or **bang** which means older brother. *(Indonesian variant – older brother)*
1.6	This is [from] the Betawi [language] or...
1.7	Or for someone thats coming [comes] from Jakarta.

Figure 2: **Participant Sample 1 - Eiphel Mercedec.** This teacher grew up in Jakarta, speaking Mandarin and Cantonese at home, Mandarin and English in education settings, and Jakartan Indonesian in community settings. This study assessed her Indonesian accent to be Jakartan, and her English as mixing aspects of Hong Kong, Singaporean, American, and Australian accents. Here the participant demonstrated some of the linguistic stance-taking described by Abtahian et al. (2021), as she explained various address terms or substitutions for English 'you' appropriate in a market in Jakarta when buying an iPhone. [ ] – square brackets are additions from the transcriber to clarify meaning. ( ) – are translations and notes on linguistic and audio features. Underlined text is in a language other than standard Indonesian or English

Claims of state-of-the-art performance from fine-tuning a pretrained ASR model with as little as 10 minutes of labelled data (Baevski et al., 2020) often depend on large-vocabulary language models (San et al., 2023). For contexts where matching language models are not readily available, more realistic results are to be expected, such as in Coto-Solano et al. (2022) where median word error rate (WER) ranged from 18-66% for Cook Islands Maori. Even with language models, WERs remained high for low-resource languages: 32.91% for read speech in Bemba language in Sikasote and Anastasopoulos (2022) and 48% for Kurmanji Kurdish in Gupta and Boulianne (2022).

The aim of this study was to achieve a useful level of accuracy in machine transcription, creating drafts for human correction to expand the Online Indonesian Learning Dataset (OIL) (Maxwell-Smith, 2023). The study used the Elpis ASR toolkit to fine-tune models with a small set of human transcribed data. We trialled different base models, parameters, and mixes of fine-tuning data against various evaluation measures to better understand the performance of the tools and achieve this goal.

The rest of the paper is organised as follows: We begin with sociolinguistic and language-teaching commentary on the data, and then provide information about the experiment design, fine-tuning parameters, and standardised results. We discuss how different models performed on audio from new lessons and for different speakers. Finally, we reflect on technologies guided by direct and indirect user need, especially how evaluation measures inform decisions about usability of machine transcription for downstream tasks such as inference editing.

2 Methodology

The experiments used Elpis, a tool to aid linguists to apply sophisticated ASR tools and approaches such as Kaldi (Povey et al., 2011), Wav2Vec2 (Baevski et al., 2020). Elpis enabled us to work with ASR base models that are available on the Hugging Face Hub[1], a repository of public and private datasets and models suitable for machine learning. Models trained in Elpis were uploaded to the Hugging Face Hub, and then used for subsequent analysis.

An initial dataset of manually transcribed audio from YouTube videos totalled 1 hour and 35 min-

[1]See github.com/CoEDL/elpis & huggingface.co

utes (19 lessons). This initial dataset was used to fine-tune ASR base models. Inference texts from an additional seven lessons were used as a draft for human editors to expand the corpus to 2 hours and 13 minutes (26 lessons) of transcribed data.

We used a mixed methods approach to analyse our results, supplementing standardised ASR evaluation with qualitative commentary on transcription workflow and corpus analysis.

Table 1: Fine-Tuned Models: Epochs and WER

Model	Epochs	WER
fb_all	40	36.95
fb_NatInd	40	40.95
fb_JER_e60	60	**30.39**
ind_nlp_all	40	**36.89**
ind_nlp_NatInd	40	41.46
ind_nlp_JER_e60	60	**32.51**

Prefix *'fb_'* used base model Wav2Vec2-XLSR-53 and *'ind_nlp'*, Wav2Vec2-XLSR-Indonesian.

2.1 Data

YouTube channels specifying a purpose to teach Indonesian were identified using keyword searches and recommendations from professional teaching networks. The listed email on these YouTube channels was contacted, progressing from channels with more to less content, until three participants were recruited (see Table 4, Appendix A). These three channel owners confirmed their ownership of materials, and their explicit consent was obtained for their materials to be used for ASR development, language and teaching analysis, as well as sharing as both audio and audio-visual files for future research (see our Ethics Statement).

To ensure our system would be robust to future data from this setting we did not exclude data with characteristics known to be challenging for ASR. These characteristics include background noise, accented speech, task specific intonation/articulation, and frequent language mixing. By using so-called 'noisy' data, our study has provided realistic insight into the performance of ASR for the real-world task of converting teacher speech from YouTube into searchable text.

Anecdotally, we observed a high rate of repetition of sounds, words and phrases in the data. We hypothesised that this would persist throughout the data as teachers aim to present 'learnable' language. That is, the data would be influenced by a common intention among teachers to present 'comprehensible input' to students (Krashen, 1981).

The language background of participants was gained via interviews, with all participants having spoken languages other than Indonesian as children. Participants reported varied language backgrounds and daily use of Indonesian at the time they filmed their videos. In their interviews, the teachers self-described their projected YouTube identity and indicated that they varied their content, tone, and language choice from video to video. Their projected identities varied and were described as 'friend', 'teacher/educator' and 'entertainer'. Participant teaching experience ranged from many years of paid work teaching Indonesian, to no experience as a professional teacher.

Almost all videos contain a mix of languages, with some dominated by Indonesian or English. Some videos explicitly focused on variation in Indonesian or words from other languages which are commonly mixed into Indonesian by speakers. Table 5 (Appendix D) contains notes on the main languages in each file, as well as a subjective comment on whether language mixing tended towards inter-utterance or intra-utterance mixing.

Noise levels were variable according to the channel and each individual video. Some videos were recorded in quiet spaces with minimal reverberation, while others have frequent high volume loudspeaker announcements from local Musholla, added sound effects, muffled voices from other speakers, and road noise. Typical noise associated with each channel is listed in Table 4 (Appendix A).

To illustrate some of the speech phenomena and other characteristics in this data we have produced a excerpt with relevant annotation (Figure 2). Examples from the two other participants are included in Appendices B and C.

2.2 Transcription

The initial transcription of files was completed by Author 1, who is an Indonesian-English bilingual, teacher, and linguist. Reference texts for each audio file were transcribed by the same transcriber using inference texts from the ASR experiments as drafts to speed the process. Reference files were checked by a second expert transcriber (Indonesian-English bilingual and linguist - see Ethics Statement below) to verify the reference transcription quality.

Transcribers erred towards recording words found in both languages with the orthography of Indonesian[2]. Non-standard forms (those not found in KBBI [3]) were transcribed as an approximation of sounds. For example '*lapan*', which is derived from '*delapan*' with first syllable deletion, and '*udah*', a Jakartan variant of '*sudah*'. Where possible, existing literature documenting variants was used to inform spelling (e.g. '*ngapain*' in Sneddon (2006)).

2.3 Experiment

The experiments consisted of fine-tuning multiple pre-trained ASR transformer models using combinations of datasets listed in Appendix D. The data in Appendix D was YouTube data manually transcribed from scratch and used to fine-tune multiple models with different characteristics. Machine transcriptions, or inference, were then used as a draft for human editing. These corrected inference files were checked by another transcriber and then considered 'gold standard' reference files, adding further data to the corpus. The original machine inference was then compared with the 'gold standard' reference files to measure WER and other performance markers. Standard ASR word error rate metrics were calculated, along with other metrics. A qualitative review of inference texts was undertaken as described in Section 3.

Fine-tuning and inference files. To enable us to select a balance of characteristics of audio and speech in our data, Author 1 listened to and coded all files from each YouTube channel for a range of characteristics (see Section 2.1 for commentary). This enabled us to choose files which roughly represented the spread of content (the topics taught and the focus of each lesson on language learning skills such as vocabulary, grammar explanation, or the teacher modelling authentic speech). We also sought to include files containing a spread of background noise and sound effects typical of channels.

When selecting files we considered speech and language behaviours such as: 1) which language dominated in a given lesson, 2) whether code-switching or translanguaging occurred between or within utterances (inter-utterance or intra-utterance), and 3) the frequency and degree of hyperarticulation by each teacher. This coding was carried out on untranscribed audio, and represented a first pass impression of audio characteristics. We sought to balance these characteristics, but note these are highly complex speech behaviours and difficult to assess even with a well-trained team of transcribers. In Maxwell-Smith et al. (2020), we discussed the complexity of measuring these behaviours in similar data at length.

2.3.1 Fine-tuning and Evaluation

Multiple models were fine-tuned to compare the effects of different combinations of data across different base models, using files manually transcribed by Author 1 (see Training Data in Appendix D). Models were evaluated using standard ASR metrics of WER from Elpis-internal train/validation/test splits for each model (see Table 1). Evaluation of inference files (see Inference Data in Appendix D) was enhanced by calculating the number of common word sequences of different lengths, and performing qualitative user rating of inference texts.

Base Models. Elpis was used to fine-tune two pre-trained base models, using combinations of labelled data for fine-tuning. One base model was Facebook's Wav2Vec2-XLSR-53 multilingual model (Conneau et al., 2021) which has been pre-trained on 56K hours of speech from 53 languages. The other base model was an Indonesian ASR model released by Indonesian NLP. Indonesian NLP used a subset of Indonesian-labelled speech from the CommonVoice dataset to fine-tune Wav2Vec2-XLSR-53, releasing it as a general Indonesian language ASR model, Wav2Vec2-XLSR-Indonesian, with 14.29% WER reported.

The base model is indicated in the first section of the model name. Models beginning with *fb_* indicates Facebook's multilingual model, and *ind_nlp_* indicates Indonesian NLP's model.

Parameters. Audio files were prepared in 16kHz, 16bit, mono, WAV format; the internal specifications used by Elpis. Transcription files were created in ELAN format, sharing a common tier name for ease of text selection in Elpis.

[2]Generally these were words loaned from English or other European languages into Indonesian.

[3]*Kamus Besar Bahasa Indonesia*, The Big Indonesian Dictionary, is produced by The Agency for Language Development and Cultivation of the Indonesian Ministry of Education, Culture, Research, and Technology.

Table 2: Inference Results for *ind_nlp*, *fb_all*, *ind_nlp_all*

Model		ind_nlp			fb_all				ind_nlp_all			
File	**Token**	**L:6**	**WER**	**CER**	**R**	**L:6**	**WER**	**CER**	**R**	**L:6**	**WER**	**CER**
EIP_010	35	1	80.00	46.07	e	1	28.57	**6.28**	e	**3**	**22.86**	6.81
EIP_011	598	0	79.93	42.03	r	**15**	**43.65**	**13.78**	e	11	46.82	15.05
EIP_013	629	1	83.47	42.86	e	**20**	44.36	**14.60**	e	**20**	**43.40**	15.97
GUN_004_01	654	1	73.70	38.07	e	**26**	**28.75**	**10.05**	e	**26**	31.65	11.20
GUN_004_10	847	6	83.47	46.74	e	**29**	41.20	13.64	e	27	**35.42**	**13.35**
JER_019	333	1	87.09	51.54	e	**14**	**33.33**	**10.98**	e	7	37.84	15.59
JER_079	992	0	94.05	54.01	e	**47**	**36.29**	**13.33**	r	34	43.45	16.32

L:6 — The number of correct word sequences of length 6 and above.
R — A human transcriber rating for the perceived usefulness of the inference as a basis for editing. Inferences rated 'e' would be edited, 'r' would be used as a reference while transcribing from scratch.
Bold scores — Best or equal best score. Table 6 in Appendix E includes results for all models in Table 1.

Preliminary rounds of fine-tuning with subsets of the data were used to identify suitable learning rates, ideal number of epochs, and batch size. Reductions in WER and loss for training conducted over 40 epochs were negligible. A trade-off was made to limit the number of epochs to reduce training time, possibly at the expense of very minor improvements in WER. A range of learning rates were used in preliminary rounds, with 1e−4 determined to be the most suitable for the final models.

Verification. After being trained, the fine-tuned Elpis models were uploaded to the Hugging Face Hub and used in Google Colab[4] to obtain inferences for untranscribed audio. Using Colab was a workaround for restrictions on the length of inference audio which Elpis would process at the time of the experiment. A custom Python script was used in Colab to load Elpis-trained models from Hugging Face and run inferencing with Hugging Face pipeline tools. Colab was later used to run evaluation scripts to calculate word and character error rates, and to find the longest correct word sequences for these inferences.

Evaluation. WER values up to 30% were reported by Gaur et al. (2016) as being useful as a 'canvas' or starting point for correction. However, due to the intricacies of manually editing transcription files in ELAN, an inference with WER within this threshold might still be cumbersome to correct, while inference outside this threshold might actually have extended sections of correct transcription. From Author 1's personal experience, editing text with frequently alternating correct/incorrect sequences was known to be more labour-intensive than editing text with long sequences of correct words, indicating that the standard WER metric of performance does not necessarily correlate with user experience.

Before reference transcriptions had been created, Author 1 made a qualitative review of inference from models that had low WER. Inference output was reviewed and rated according to the estimated frequency of extended sequences of correct words, as well as the position of necessary edits and the number of keystrokes required to correct the text in ELAN. Based on this assessment of the anticipated manipulation process, a rating for each inference text was made from a five-point scale (useless, glance, refer, edit, wow).

3 Results

The speaker specific models *fb_JER_e60* and *nlp_all_JER_e60* achieved the lowest WER from elpis-internal train/test splits (30.39% and 32.51% respectively). Train/test evaluation is compared in Table 1. The initial results from *fb_JER_e60* and *nlp_all_JER_e60* may have been due to the greater number of epochs. However, the performance of the models when trained was not reflected in their application to new lessons from the same speaker (WERs of 38.44% and 44.36% from *fb_JER_e60*).

[4]https://colab.research.google.com

The next best training evaluation scores were from models fine-tuned with all our data: *ind_nlp_all* and *fb_all*[5]. Experimental models fine-tuned with a subset of data[6] from teachers who were long-term residents of Indonesia (models with suffix *_NatInd*) had higher WER.

While Indonesian NLP reports WER of 14.29% for the base model *ind_nlp*, it did not score well on inference of our multilingual audio (Table 2 sets out evaluation metrics for inference of new lesson audio). No WER below 70% was achieved using *ind_nlp* and very few long correct sequences were produced. Using Indonesian NLP's model, which is fine-tuned with monolingual Indonesian data, was not suitable for our data.

Our own fine-tuned models were a dramatic improvement on these results. The best WERs on inference files ranged from 22.86% to 43.65%. No single model consistently achieved the best WER, CER or correct sequence of six or more on inference of new audio (Table 2). The *fb_all* model achieved a greater number of better scores, and on closer inspection of correct sequence counts would appear to have produced inference which is more easily editable (Table 3). Merged word errors, such as *'ribuseratus'* rather than *'ribu seratus'* (thousand one hundred), were prevalent in inference from all models.

Table 3: Correct word sequences in inference from *fb_all* and *ind_nlp_all* models

	fb_all				**ind_nlp_all**			
File	**L:4**	**L:5**	**L:6**	**L:7**	**L:4**	**L:5**	**L:6**	**L:7**
EIP_010	2	1	1	1	3	3	3	2
EIP_011	31	24	15	12	28	19	11	10
EIP_013	39	30	20	17	31	28	20	17
GUN_004_01	42	34	26	22	39	32	26	16
GUN_004_10	51	41	29	26	52	39	27	19
JER_019	18	17	14	10	18	14	7	6
JER_079	85	68	47	36	77	52	34	26

L:x — The number of correct word sequences of length x is marked with L:x.

Two files from participant Jeremy Snyder (JER), received best scores with the Facebook base model fine-tuned on all data (*fb_all*). Data from other participants achieved better scores across both the *fb_all* and *ind_nlp_all* models. Jeremy was the only participant with English as a first language. This weighting towards the Facebook base model may be related to Jeremy's spoken English more closely matching English in the Facebook base model data.

Qualitative human rating of inference indicated inferences from *fb_all* and *ind_nlp_all* were suitable for editing (see R in Table 2). Verifying this finding with timed transcription experiments to ascertain the degree of acceleration was beyond the scope of this project. However, the suitability of inference files for editing was confirmed by Author 1 as she used them to expand the dataset. The process of editing inference also led to interesting reflections on the data itself, as discussed below.

4 Discussion

Principal findings. This paper makes a unique contribution in demonstrating the viability of using ASR for an explicit and executed purpose. Machine transcription was successfully edited to increase the size of a noisy, mixed-language, Indonesian-English, YouTube language teaching dataset with three speakers. The expanded dataset will improve analysis of teacher speech by a teacher-researcher. It also provides ethically sourced and openly released materials to engineer and enhance bespoke NLP solutions in a setting that is currently low-resource.

While machine transcription accelerated the transcription process, the process of fine-tuning base models and preparing data required an upfront investment which was not compensated for by this acceleration over seven inference files. We hope that our upfront investment can be useful to others via our models and data on Hugging Face.

The process of editing machine transcriptions revealed workflow and evaluation needs. It also impacted human transcriber interpretation of the data, provoking discussion of how multilingual, accented, language teaching plays out. Meanwhile, so-called 'errors' in inference were less concerning than they would be in other fields where accuracy is of paramount importance (such as in medical applications of ASR (Joseph et al., 2020; Miner et al., 2020).

[5](Maxwell-Smith and Foley, 2023b) & (Maxwell-Smith and Foley, 2023a)

[6]See data marked with [a] in Appendix D

balken tut	balkantut	kento	kentoot	**saya** kentuc
bau kentut	bau kentut	kentut	kentut	kentut

Figure 3: Incorrect inference (Green) and reference (Red) of a lesson using fart humour to teach grammar. Reference transcription is: *bau kentut* (fart stench), *bau kentut* (fart stench), *kentut* (fart), *kentut* (fart), *saya kentut* (I farted)

Inference:	the	adde	of the	food	the back	age	of the	sood	it is called
Reference:		edge		foot		edge		foot	

Figure 4: Insights into accented speech via error correction of inference.

Correct sequences: length and location. The placement of correct sequences of inference influenced the usability of an inference as an editable draft. Specifically, longer correct sequences and those that were left-aligned reduced the time spent editing, an impact not measured by WER. Similarly, word final spelling errors were less disruptive to the editing process as they required less keystrokes to correct. As an example, for reference *'satu ribu'*, the inference *'a satu ribu'* is more disruptive than *'satu ribua a'*. This is despite having lower WER and CER.

'Out-of-domain' lexicon. In a lesson using humorous discussion of farts to teach grammar, Jeremy Snyder produces the words *'bau'* (stench) and *'kentut'* (fart) repeatedly. These are consistently inferred incorrectly (see Figure 3), despite minimal hyperarticulation and background noise, and fairly clear articulation. This is likely due to their absence from training data — they belong to language rarely used in public settings though they are not uncommon in everyday life[7]. Reflecting on this limitation of machine transcription highlights the domain of use for certain language and how students may encounter, or not encounter, certain words in their learning journey.

Accented speech. The reflection of speech behaviours in machine transcription also stimulated reflection on teacher pronunciation. The use of context and language knowledge in understanding and interpreting teacher speech is highlighted in the following examples.

In a lesson from Gunawan Tambunsaribu (GUN) the word final 't' in 'foot' was converted to a 'd' in the machine inference (see Figure 4). Human analysis found the production of 'oo' (in 'foot') by the participant matched with the common grapheme to phoneme pair in words like 'too' and 'roo'. However, 'foot', confusingly given it's spelling, is pronounced like 'put'. The inference highlighted the transfer of Indonesian vowel production and possibly a speech error resulting from irregularities in orthographic conventions in English.

Similar to a language model (LM), a human transcriber editing the inference in Figure 4 would step through each word, finding 'adde' to be a non-word. Presuming correction to 'edge' was substituted, the sentence 'The edge of the food' would be judged improbable and corrected despite the vowel production described in the previous paragraph. Further, a human and a LM would preference 'foot' over 'food' as the preceding data indicates body parts are likely, being the topic of the lesson.

In another inference, the transcription of 'tv' as 'tipi' matched the participant's production of the word. The inference reflected a common characteristic displayed by Indonesian speakers in which fricatives and plosives[8] are not always differentiated (Nurhayati, 2020).

'Non-words'. The machine transcription of 'non-words', or words invented by the teacher to illustrate a point, also spurred discussion and reflection. For example, data, again from Gunawan Tambunsaribu, in which he purposefully produced 'yuk' incorrectly with the glottal stop aspirated was inferred as 'youk'. This estimated orthography for a non-existent word was found stimulating for transcribers rather than harmful.

[7]This is not a comment on the authors' own level of flatulence, though it is relevant to the topic of domain shift in computational linguistics (Paraskevopoulos et al., 2023).

[8]In this example (/v/) and (/p/) respectively.

Editing inference 'errors' highlighted patterns in teachers' speech and illustrated incidental learning encountered by students. All participants demonstrated non-standard pronunciation of Indonesian and English. The examples above offer evidence for the role of intermediary targets of pronunciation in language teaching and techniques in pronunciation instruction; a lively research area in second language acquisition (Lee et al., 2014).

Language models. Often the addition of a LM will be used to improve ASR and other NLP. However, in this application of ASR, introducing a LM would be unlikely to assist as code-switching behaviours, non-standard grammar and accents, as well as situated language from the language learning setting has largely been excluded from language technologies (Scao et al., 2022). In other words, LMs built from data similar to ours are not yet available.

In our study, human transcribers took on the role of LM correction. However, this placed signficant demands on transcribers to be multilingual and knowledgeable in the language learning setting. These demands make transcription and error correction of this data a true bottleneck. Optimistically perhaps, we see this work as potentially enriching for teachers and their reflective teaching practice. It can bring attention to interlanguage and movement between native speaker modelling and intermediary productions of sounds and language structures.

Future work. ASR systems fine-tuned with very small quantities of data often rely on LMs trained with large amounts of text data (San et al., 2023). These systems typically use a multilingual base model that has been fine-tuned to a monolingual language, with a monolingual LM[9]. In this setting, further work to develop a complex multilingual LM could improve results with a pre-trained multilingual model fine-tuned with multilingual data.

A major challenge in the development of multilingual LMs for contexts such as this is the varying inter-utterance and intra-utterance code-switching that occurs in teacher speech (Maxwell-Smith et al., 2020). These switches are likely to disrupt potential identification of language for an n-gram LM. An n-gram sequence identified as English may in fact erroneously negate a correctly identified Indonesian word in the sequence.

Further work to investigate initial diarisation/language identification may be a fruitful approach to handling this language complexity. Such an approach was taken in Szalay et al. (2022) to assist with mixed data from adult and child speakers. In this setting, multiple mono-lingual LMs used on identified languages and then compiled could be helpful (Shen, 2022). However, with the degree of hyperarticulation and accent evident in this study's audio, reliable language identification itself is likely to be difficult.

The prevalence of merged word errors identified in inference texts (e.g. 'reduplicationand' rather than 'reduplication and'), would be resolved in a monolingual system through the use of a LM. Given a LM may not work well on data like this, future work for complex language systems could investigate the benefits of a rudimentary splitting step based on matches with combined bigrams or trigrams from a multilingual vocabulary list.

Audio content analysis indicates that errors concentrated at the beginning and ends of files were associated with background music. Given the consistent poor inference text in these sections, better performance would be likely by excluding these sections of the files.

5 Conclusion

Our findings offer a reality check of ASR performance with 'difficult' data, including newer techniques of transfer learning. Our results clearly indicated that publicly available models for Indonesian are not suitable for processing holistic language teaching data. Inference from a model fine-tuned on a small dataset of complex language was much more useful. The WER remained high, however, rather than discarding results based on the industry-standard/internal expectations, we persisted and edited inference text to expand our dataset. The resulting insights into user workflows encourage investigation of task-specific evaluation measures. Meanwhile, insights into data characteristics that were highlighted by editing the inference texts go some way to counterbalancing the time spent in interactions with ASR output by language-teaching professionals. Our ethically sourced dataset[10] and best models[11] are available on Hugging Face.

[9] https://discuss.huggingface.co/t/how-to-create-wav2vec2-with-language-model/12703

[10] Online Indonesian Learning (OIL) Dataset

[11] OIL ASR models

Limitations

This study represented complex human language with simple orthography, including language mixing, hyperarticulation and variation. Further linguistic annotation would enrich the dataset and enable deeper insights into language teaching behaviours. For example, phonetic transcription would help to differentiate words that occur in both languages and allow for exploration and comparison of accented speech between participants.

The potential benefits of using a multilingual LM to improve ASR results were not studied due to the language complexities of the dataset. Further work is required to: 1) develop complex multilingual LMs matching the language and, 2) conduct subsequent studies on the efficacy of a complex LM in the ASR system.

Ethics Statement

The audio (and visual) data from the three YouTube channels was transferred by participants after discussing the project and possible impacts of sharing their data (Ethics Approval No. 2017/889 of the *Australian National University* Human Research Committee, *Speech Recognition; Building Datasets from Indonesian Language Classrooms and Resources* protocol). Files were screened for intelligible speech from people other than the participant and those containing such data were removed from the dataset. The non-author transcriber referred to in Section 2 completed the transcription as part of an exchange of editing and proof reading. Our appreciation for his contribution to the project is expressed in our Acknowledgements.

With a view to advancing the language technologies available for Indonesian, and especially Indonesian and English bilingual data, and to support research into Indonesian language teaching, the dataset has been made available for other researchers to further develop these tools and complete their own analysis. Our study documented one approach to developing NLP in understudied language situations, contributing to realistic expectations of NLP in settings outside monolingual English settings most supported by the investment of business interests.

The study and release of data does embody some risks for participants as data stored in an open repository could be downloaded to create other derivative works not aligned with this research (Kale 2019). As videos contain the professional teaching practice of some participants, and the 'YouTuber' persona of others, there is a risk of reputational damage. This risk and that of derivative works was made clear in the participant information sheet and storage in an open repository was subject to explicit consent on the consent form. To further reduce risk, videos with individuals not explicitly involved in the making of the video (bystanders) were excluded from the dataset. We believe the risk of misappropriation of content from YouTube was already significant for participants as their work could be copied relatively easily from YouTube; their involvement in this project increased the risk of misappropriation only slightly.

Acknowledgements

We would like to acknowledge the support and guidance of our supervisors Janet Wiles, Professor Hanna Suominen, Dr Michelle Kohler, and Assoc Professor Danielle Barth, and colleagues Nay San and Daan van Esch. Our special thanks to our research participants, Gunawan Tambunsaribu, Jeremy Snyder, and Eiphel Mercedec, and to Yustinus Ghanggo Ate for contributing his expertise and time in our editing exchange.

References

Maya Ravindranath Abtahian, Abigail C. Cohn, Dwi Noverini Djenar, and Rachel C. Vogel. 2021. Jakarta indonesian first-person singular pronouns: Form, function and variation. *Asia-Pacific Language Variation*, 7(2):185–214.

Alexei Baevski, Henry Zhou, Abdelrahman Mohamed, and Michael Auli. 2020. wav2vec 2.0: A framework for self-supervised learning of speech representations. *CoRR*, abs/2006.11477.

Abeba Birhane, Pratyusha Kalluri, Dallas Card, William Agnew, Ravit Dotan, and Michelle Bao. 2022. The values encoded in machine learning research. In *2022 ACM Conference on Fairness, Accountability, and Transparency*, FAccT '22, page 173–184, New York, NY, USA. Association for Computing Machinery.

Judith Bishop. 2022. *Linguistic Diversity in AI: A Provocation.* ARC Centre of Excellence for the Dynamics of Language, Panel: New connections for language and technology CoEDL End-of-Centre Event, Friday, 30 September 2022.

Kenneth Ward Church, Zeyu Chen, and Yanjun Ma. 2021. Emerging trends: A gentle introduction to fine-tuning. *Natural Language Engineering*, 27(6):763–778.

Alexis Conneau, Alexei Baevski, Ronan Collobert, Abdelrahman Mohamed, and Michael Auli. 2021. Unsupervised cross-lingual representation learning for speech recognition. In *Interspeech*. ISCA.

Rolando Coto-Solano, Sally Akevai Nicholas, Samiha Datta, Victoria Quint, Piripi Wills, Emma Ngakuravaru Powell, Liam Koka'ua, Syed Tanveer, and Isaac Feldman. 2022. Development of automatic speech recognition for the documentation of Cook Islands Māori. In *Proceedings of the Thirteenth Language Resources and Evaluation Conference*, pages 3872–3882, Marseille, France. European Language Resources Association.

Fahim Faisal, Sharlina Keshava, Md Mahfuz Ibn Alam, and Antonios Anastasopoulos. 2021. SD-QA: Spoken dialectal question answering for the real world. In *Findings of the Association for Computational Linguistics: EMNLP 2021*, pages 3296–3315, Punta Cana, Dominican Republic. Association for Computational Linguistics.

Yashesh Gaur, Walter S. Lasecki, Florian Metze, and Jeffrey P. Bigham. 2016. The effects of automatic speech recognition quality on human transcription latency. In *Proceedings of the 13th International Web for All Conference*, W4A '16, New York, NY, USA. Association for Computing Machinery.

Vishwa Gupta and Gilles Boulianne. 2022. Progress in multilingual speech recognition for low resource languages Kurmanji Kurdish, Cree and inuktut. In *Proceedings of the Thirteenth Language Resources and Evaluation Conference*, pages 6420–6428, Marseille, France. European Language Resources Association.

Joseph Joseph, Zena EH Moore, Declan Patton, Tom O'Connor, and Linda Elizabeth Nugent. 2020. The impact of implementing speech recognition technology on the accuracy and efficiency (time to complete) clinical documentation by nurses: A systematic review. *Journal of Clinical Nursing*, 29(13-14):2125–2137.

Daniel Jurafsky and James H Martin. 2023. Automatic Speech Recognition and Text-to-Speech. In *Speech and Language Processing*.

Allison Koenecke, Andrew Nam, Emily Lake, Joe Nudell, Minnie Quartey, Zion Mengesha, Connor Toups, John R. Rickford, Dan Jurafsky, and Sharad Goel. 2020. Racial disparities in automated speech recognition. *Proceedings of the National Academy of Sciences*, 117(14):7684–7689.

Stephen Krashen. 1981. *Second Language Acquisition and Second Language Learning*. Pergamon Press Inc.

Junkyu Lee, Juhyun Jang, and Luke Plonsky. 2014. The Effectiveness of Second Language Pronunciation Instruction: A Meta-Analysis. *Applied Linguistics*, 36(3):345–366.

Zara Maxwell-Smith. 2023. Online Indonesian Learning dataset (OIL) (revision b2a39e5).

Zara Maxwell-Smith and Ben Foley. 2023a. ZMaxwell-Smith/OIL_YT_fb_all Automatic Speech Recognition (ASR) model (revision 1fb3a19).

Zara Maxwell-Smith and Ben Foley. 2023b. ZMaxwell-Smith/OIL_YT_ind_nlp_all Automatic Speech Recognition (ASR) model (revision 1a14ec0).

Zara Maxwell-Smith, Simón González Ochoa, Ben Foley, and Hanna Suominen. 2020. Applications of natural language processing in bilingual language teaching: an indonesian-english case study. In *Proceedings of the Fifteenth Workshop on Innovative Use of NLP for Building Educational Applications*, pages 124–134.

Adam S Miner, Albert Haque, Jason A Fries, Scott L Fleming, Denise E Wilfley, G Terence Wilson, Arnold Milstein, Dan Jurafsky, Bruce A Arnow, W Stewart Agras, et al. 2020. Assessing the accuracy of automatic speech recognition for psychotherapy. *NPJ Digital Medicine*, 3(1):1–8.

Dwi Nurhayati. 2020. Plosive and fricative sounds produced by efl students using online media: A perspective on learning english phonology. In *Proceedings of the 1st International Conference on Folklore, Language, Education and Exhibition (ICOFLEX 2019)*.

Georgios Paraskevopoulos, Theodoros Kouzelis, Georgios Rouvalis, Athanasios Katsamanis, Vassilis Katsouros, and Alexandros Potamianos. 2023. Sample-efficient unsupervised domain adaptation of speech recognition systems a case study for Modern Greek.

Daniel Povey, Arnab Ghoshal, Gilles Boulianne, Lukas Burget, Ondrej Glembek, Nagendra Goel, Mirko Hannemann, Petr Motlicek, Yanmin Qian, Petr Schwarz, Jan Silovsky, Georg Stemmer, and Karel Vesely. 2011. The Kaldi speech recognition toolkit. In *IEEE 2011 Workshop on Automatic Speech Recognition and Understanding*. IEEE Signal Processing Society. IEEE Catalog No.: CFP11SRW-USB.

Nay San, Martijn Bartelds, Blaine Billings, Ella de Falco, Hendi Feriza, Johan Safri, Wawan Sahrozi, Ben Foley, Bradley McDonnell, and Dan Jurafsky. 2023. Leveraging supplementary text data to kick-start automatic speech recognition system development with limited transcriptions. In *Proceedings of the Sixth Workshop on the Use of Computational Methods in the Study of Endangered Languages*.

Teven Le Scao, Angela Fan, Christopher Akiki, Ellie Pavlick, Suzana Ilić, Daniel Hesslow, Roman Castagné, Alexandra Sasha Luccioni, François Yvon, Matthias Gallé, et al. 2022. Bloom: A 176b-parameter open-access multilingual language model. *ArXiv*, abs/2211.05100.

Gaofei Shen. 2022. Does where words come from matter? Leveraging self-supervised models for multilingual ASR and LID. Master's thesis, Center for Information Technology of the University of Groningen, Campus Fryslan, August.

Claytone Sikasote and Antonios Anastasopoulos. 2022. BembaSpeech: A speech recognition corpus for the Bemba language. In *Proceedings of the Thirteenth Language Resources and Evaluation Conference*, pages 7277–7283, Marseille, France. European Language Resources Association.

James N. Sneddon. 2006. *Colloquial Jakartan Indonesian*, volume 581. Pacific Linguistics, Research School of Pacific and Asian Studies, Australian National University, Canberra.

Tünde Szalay, Louise Ratko, Mostafa Shahin, Tharmakulasingam Sirojan, Kirrie Ballard, Felicity Cox, and Beena Ahmed. 2022. A semi-automatic workflow for orthographic transcription of a novel speech corpus: A case study of AusKidTalk. In *Proceedings of the Eighteenth Australasian International Conference on Speech Science and Technology*. Australasian Speech Science and Technology Association.

Appendix A Speaker/channel characteristics

Table 4: Speaker/channel characteristics

Eiphel Mercedec	**Gunawan Tambunsaribu**	**Jeremy Snyder**
5-Minute Indonesian	Indonesian Language for Beginners ENG-INA	Dua Budaya
Languages used at home		
Mandarin, Cantonese, Indonesian, English	Batak Simalungun, other varieties of Batak	English, Indonesian
Language of formal education		
Mandarin, English	Indonesian, English	English, Indonesian
Use of Indonesian		
Community interactions	Family, work, community	Teaching, family interactions
Residency		
Indonesia, Jakarta	Indonesia, Jakarta	Australia, Perth
Typical 'noise' in audio		
Clear, music, sound effects	Background noise (call to prayer, other speakers, street noise)	Clear, some music
Duration		
34 minutes	7 hours 51 minutes	2 hours 53 minutes
Number of files		
13	22	63

Characteristics: This table is characteristics drawn from participant descriptions of their lives at the time of video/channel creation.

Appendix B Speaker sample 2

Data sample 2 - Participant Gunawan Tambunsaribu	
2.1	The edge of the foot. *(banging) (unintelligible children's voices) (foot is produced with /u:/)*
2.2	The back edge of the foot. *(foot is produced with /u:/)*
2.3	It is called **tumit** *(heel).* *(child yells)*
2.4	**Tumit** *(heel).*
2.5	In English heel.
2.7	Heel.
2.8	In **Bahasa Indonesia** *(Indonesian language it is)* **tumit** *(heel).*
2.9	And then here this is stomach. *(child yells loudly) (stomach is produced with word final /tʃ/)*
2.10	Stomach.
2.11	Stomach in **Bahasa Indonesia peerruut ya** *(the Indonesian language is stomach, okay)?* *(short yell from child) (hyperarticulation)*
2.12	**Peeeerrruuut**[a] *(stomach).* *(unintelligible children's voices) (word is extremely hyperarticulated)*
2.13	**Ya?**
2.14	**Peeerruut**[b] *(stomach).* *(unintelligible children speaking) (hyperarticulation)*
2.15	**Peerruut** *(stomach).* *(hyperarticulation)*
2.16	**Ya?**
2.17	Stomach.

Figure 5: **Participant Sample 2 - Gunawan Tambunsaribu.** This teacher grew up speaking Batak Simalungun, completed his education in Indonesian and English and has lived in Jakarta for more than 15 years, speaking Indonesian and Betawi. His Indonesian accent is Jakartan, while his English could be described as having an international and Indonesian accent. Here he produces hyperarticulated speech to highlight the sounds of new vocabulary. The duration of the most hyperarticulated instance of 'perut" is perut[a], (1.4 seconds). While still hyperarticulated, perut[b] is much shorter (0.84 seconds). The token 'stomach' is transcribed orthographically here but varies, with the first instance produced with a 'tch' sound, as in 'latch' which is then corrected by the participant. The audio includes background noise from children playing and unintelligible childrens' speech. ( ) – are translations and notes on linguistic and audio features. / / - provide phonetic information.

Appendix C Speaker sample 3

Data sample 3 - Participant Jeremy Snyder	
3.1	In Indonesian **tidak** *(not)* negates verbs or adjectives but **bukan** *(not)* negates nouns. *(Indonesian is hyperarticulated and stressed) (glottal stop in tidak is aspirated)*
3.2	You need to be **hati-hati** *(careful)* when using **bukan** *(not)* and **tidak** *(not).* *(Indonesian is hyperarticulated and stressed) (glottal stop in tidak is aspirated)*
3.3	For example...
3.4	**Saya bukan kentut** *(I'm not a fart).* *(Hyperarticulated and stressed)*
3.5	Makes **kentut** *(the word fart)* into a thing. *(Indonesian is hyperarticulated and stressed)*
3.6	So it means, I am not a fart.
3.7	If you add in the word **yang** *(determiner - the one who)* it changes the meaning again. *(Indonesian is hyperarticulated and stressed)*
3.8	**Saya bukan yang kentut** *(I'm not the one who farted).* *(Hyperarticulated and stressed)*

Figure 6: **Participant Sample 3 - Jeremy Snyder.** This teacher grew up speaking English, completed his education in English and Indonesian, and has lived in Australia and Indonesia, speaking English and Indonesian. His Indonesian has an Australian accent, as does his English. In this example he produces hyperarticulated speech to highlight the sounds of target language for learners and for emphasis/comedic effect.( ) – are translations and notes on linguistic and audio features.

Appendix D Datasets

Table 5: Datasets

File name	Duration	Language	Codeswitch	Music	Audio quality	Hyper
			TRAINING DATA			
Eiphel						
EIP_002 [a]	0:01:46	Mix	Intra	X	Moderate	High
EIP_003 [a]	0:02:09	Mix	Intra	X	Moderate	High
EIP_006 [a]	0:02:45	Mix	Intra	X	Moderate	Med
EIP_007 [a]	0:01:40	Mix	Inter	X	Moderate	Med
EIP_008 [a]	0:00:26	Mix	Inter	X	Moderate	Med
Subtotal:	*0:08:45*					
Gunawan						
GUN_001 [a]	0:04:27	Mix	Inter		Poor	High
GUN_002 [a]	0:05:42	Mix	Inter		Poor	Very High
GUN_005 [a]	0:05:04	Mix	Inter		Very Poor	Very High
GUN_008 [a]	0:05:37	Mix	Inter		Moderate	Med
GUN_011 [a]	0:33:28	Mix	Inter		Very Poor	Very High
GUN_022 [a]	0:03:44	Mix	Inter		Poor	Very High
Subtotal:	*0:58:03*					
Jeremy						
JER_004 [b]	0:01:38	Mix	Inter	X	Good	Min
JER_013 [b]	0:02:02	Eng	Inter	X	Good	Med
JER_017 [b]	0:01:25	Mix	Inter	X	Good	Min
JER_020 [b]	0:01:25	Mix	Intra	X	Good	Med
JER_049 [b]	0:05:18	Eng	Intra	X	Moderate	High
JER_050 [b]	0:06:06	Eng	Inter	X	Moderate	Med
JER_051 [b]	0:07:13	Eng	Inter	X	Moderate	Med
JER_109 [b]	0:03:29	Ind	na	X	Poor	Med
Subtotal:	*0:28:38*					
Total training:	**1:35:26**					
			INFERENCE DATA			
EIP_010	0:00:26	Mix	Inter	X	Moderate	Low
EIP_011	0:00:26	Mix	Inter	X	Moderate	Low
EIP_013	0:04:48	Mix	Inter	X	Moderate	Med
GUN_004_01	0:08:00	Mix	Inter		Moderate	High
GUN_004_10	0:08:00	Mix	Inter		Moderate	High
JER_019	0:03:07	Mix	Intra	X	Moderate	Med
JER_079	0:08:59	Mix	Intra	X	Good	Low
Total inference:	**0:37:45**					

[a] Subset of files used to fine-tune the *fb_NatInd* and *ind_nlp_NatInd* models.
[b] Subset of files used to fine-tune the *fb_JER_e60* and *ind_nlp_JER_e60* models.
Files are identified using part of their filename: E.g. EIP_002 refers to ZMS_EIP_002_L1-Alpha.wav.
Codes: *Language* - the dominant language, *Codeswitch* - whether inter- or intra-utterance switches appeared more common, *Audio quality* - a subjective judgement of 'noise' (call to prayer, unintelligible voices from other speakers, chickens, etc.), *Hyper* - the prevalence and degree of hyper-articulation.

Appendix E Extended Results

Table 6: Extended Inference Results

File	EIP_010	EIP_011	EIP_013	GUN_004_01	GUN_004_10	JER_019	JER_079
Words	35	598	629	654	847	333	992
Time	0:26	4:48	4:25	8:00	8:00	3:07	8:59
				ind_nlp			
L:6	1	0	1	1	6	1	0
WER	80.00	79.93	83.47	73.70	83.47	87.09	94.05
CER	46.07	42.03	42.86	38.07	46.74	51.54	54.01
				fb_all			
R	e	r	e	e	e	e	e
L:6	1	15	20	26	29	14	47
WER	28.57	43.65	44.36	28.75	41.20	33.33	36.29
CER	6.28	13.78	14.60	10.05	13.64	10.98	13.33
				ind_nlp_all			
R	e	e	e	e	e	e	r
L:6	3	11	20	26	27	7	34
WER	22.86	46.82	43.40	31.65	35.42	37.84	43.45
CER	6.81	15.05	15.97	11.20	13.35	15.59	16.32
				fb_nat_ind			
L:6	1	14	13	22	26	4	17
WER	31.43	52.51	46.42	33.18	43.09	65.47	51.82
CER	8.90	17.84	15.91	10.74	15.50	24.09	18.52
				ind_nlp_nat_ind			
L:6	0	4	13	25	24	4	8
WER	42.86	52.01	47.38	32.42	41.20	62.76	60.69
CER	10.47	18.25	18.25	11.72	15.32	28.49	26.39
				fb_JER_e60			
L:6	-	-	-	-	-	7	22
WER	-	-	-	-	-	38.44	44.36
CER	-	-	-	-	-	13.28	15.41
				ind_nlp_JER_e60			
R	-	-	-	-	-	e	r
L:6	-	-	-	-	-	13	27
WER	-	-	-	-	-	40.24	45.67
CER	-	-	-	-	-	18.94	18.56

Colour — Coloured cells indicate best or equal best scores.
R — A rating given by a human transcriber for the perceived usefulness of the inference as a basis for editing. Inferences rated 'e' would be edited, and 'r' used as a reference while transcribing from scratch.
L:6 — The number of correct word sequences of length 6 and above.

Application of Speech Processes for the Documentation of Kréyòl Gwadloupéyen

Éric Le Ferrand[1,2], **Fabiola Henri**[3], **Benjamin Lecouteux**[2], **Emmanuel Schang** [1]
[1]LLL, Université d'Orléans, [2]LIG, Université Grenoble Alpes, France
[3]University at Buffalo, USA

Abstract

In recent times, there has been a growing number of research studies focused on addressing the challenges posed by low-resource languages and the transcription bottleneck phenomenon. This phenomenon has driven the development of speech recognition methods to transcribe regional and Indigenous languages automatically. Although there is much talk about bridging the gap between speech technologies and field linguistics, there is a lack of documented efficient communication between NLP experts and documentary linguists. The models created for low-resource languages often remain within the confines of computer science departments, while documentary linguistics remain attached to traditional transcription workflows. This paper presents the early stage of a collaboration between NLP experts and field linguists, resulting in the successful transcription of Kréyòl Gwadloupéyen using speech recognition technology.

1 Introduction

The fields of descriptive and documentary linguistics concentrate on gathering information and describing language phenomena. This work is typically performed on small, Indigenous, and regional languages that have a limited number of speakers. The linguist's process typically involves recording raw speech, either spontaneous or elicited, transcribing the recordings, translating them, and conducting an analysis. In this pipeline, the transcription becomes the data, but transcribing raw speech is a time-consuming task and is often seen as a bottleneck when a large amount of speech is collected but only a small portion is used.

Speech technologies have been viewed as a solution to this bottleneck issue by automatically annotating raw speech collections. Regular automatic speech recognition (ASR) has proven to be challenging due to the lack of data available in most languages to train robust models. However, alternative methods, such as spoken term detection, phone recognition, and the use of universal models, offer new possibilities for collaboration between field linguists and NLP experts.

We present here an application of speech processing on raw field linguistics recordings in Kréyòl Gwadloupéyen. Our objective has two parts: firstly, to exhibit the capability of a wav2vec and CTC-based system for our target language, and secondly, to illustrate how the transcription output can be valuable and utilised by field linguists.

2 Background

2.1 Fieldwork technologies

In the past decade, there have been ongoing discussions about developing technology for the purpose of linguistic fieldwork (Gessler, 2022; Gauthier, 2018; Moeller, 2014). The main argument has been to adapt emerging technologies such as smartphones for fieldwork. The recent improvement of speech recognition for low-resource languages has also been seen as a way to mitigate the transcription bottleneck (Himmelmann, 1998) automatically transcribing large amount of untranscribed speech data (e.g. Foley et al., 2018; Shi et al., 2021; Adams et al., 2021).

Looking at the role of technologies in the current linguistics fieldwork workflow, only a few tools are still widely used (e.g. Boersma and Weenink, 1996; Wittenburg et al., 2006). The other projects involving tools design often end up discontinued (Bird et al., 2014; Gauthier et al., 2016) or stayed at the prototype stage (Lane et al., 2021; Le Ferrand et al., 2022; Bettinson and Bird, 2017). Leveraging speech technologies for scaling up language documentation has had limited impact as well, probably because of lack of data available for low-resource languages to build robust models (Gupta and Boulianne, 2020a,b).

Proceedings of the Second Workshop on NLP Applications to Field Linguistics, pages 17–22
May 6, 2023

The recent expansion of speech recognition models based on wav2vec2.0 (Conneau et al., 2021) combined with CTC algorithms (e.g. Macaire et al., 2022) open new opportunities for low-resource languages. Such an architecture is not restricted by a language model and can produce tokens out of vocabulary.

2.2 Kréyòl gwadloupéyen

Kréyòl gwadloupéyen is spoken on Guadeloupe Island and in mainland France by approximately 800 000 speakers. Kréyòl gwadloupéyen was born in the colonial context from the contact between French settlers and African slaves in the French West Indies (see (Prudent, 1999), (Chaudenson, 2004) among others). It has historically been stigmatised and viewed as a "lesser" form of language compared to French, the language of the colonisers. In terms of language use, Kréyòl gwadloupéyen is the primary language of daily communication for a large part of the population of Guadeloupe, particularly in informal settings. French, on the other hand, is used in formal and official contexts, such as in schools, government institutions, and the media. In this context of diglossia (Jeannot-Fourcaud and Jno-Baptiste, 2008), code-mixing is frequent, which is an obvious challenge for ASR systems. In short, creole languages share most of their lexicon with the dominant language (the lexifier language), while their grammar is significantly different from the grammar of the lexifier. The origins of the grammatical differences might be a matter of debate (see (Mufwene, 1997; Velupillai, 2015) among others). To give only one example of the distance and similarities of French and Kréyòl gwadloupéyen, see (1):

(1) a. Jan pa sav palé kréyol
Jean NEG know speak creole
'Jean doesn't speak creole'

b. Jean ne sait pas parler créole
Jean NEG know NEG speak creole
'Jean doesn't speak creole'

The NSF-IRES 1952568: Experimental linguistics in the Caribbean seeks to provide students with an international experience conducting linguistic research on low-resource and under-described creole languages like Kréyòl gwadloupéyen. During this 5-7 weeks program, fellows investigate a linguistic phenomenon in Gwadloupéyen on the basis of raw data (spontaneous speech or directed interviews) they collect to contribute to the description and documentation of the language. As previously noted, one of biggest challenges for field linguists and even more so, for the NSF-IRES fellows, remains time invested with transcriptions. Often, these recordings are unexploited for lack of time, adding to the issue of under-description. Only 60min of the approximately 10 hours of recordings collected in 2022 was transcribed, and this only after the program had ended. Notwithstanding code switching/mixing, the fellows' unfamiliarity with the language's phonology made the transcription exercise arduous and lengthier.

3 Automations

3.1 Data

The ASR experiments are based on the work of Macaire et al. (2022), who used a 60-minute-long speech corpus of spontaneous speech in Kréyòl gwadloupéyen for training.

The testing data consist of several hours of raw, unsegmented, and untranscribed speech recorded during a 2022 fieldwork. The speech is spontaneous and sparse across the recording, with overlapping speech, laughters, silences, and random noises spread across the collection. The speech segments are also not necessarily in Kréyòl, and even if the limit between French and Kréyòl gwadloupéyen is not clear, some segments are clearly in French and even English. One 1-hour-long recording was selected, which, after some verification, contains a majority of segments in Kréyòl.

3.2 Preprocessing

Speech processing systems generally expect short utterances of clear speech, so the type of data described previously is not usable as is and needs to be preprocessed. Following the ideas of the sparse transcription model (Bird, 2020), we used *auditok*[1], a Voice Activity Detection tool, to filter out non-speech segments. This tool works in an unsupervised fashion, with detection based on the energy of the audio signal. Although more accurate VAD tools are available, auditok provides a good baseline for this preliminary study.

3.3 ASR and Self-supervised Learning

Self-supervised learning (SSL) is the task of learning powerful representations from huge unlabeled

[1] https://auditok.readthedocs.io/en/latest/

data to recognise and understand patterns from a less common problem. These models allows to improve performance on downstream tasks for ASR in low-resource contexts (Baevski et al., 2019; Kawakami et al., 2020). These work are based on the Wav2Vec2.0 (Baevski et al., 2020) model. It builds context representations from continuous speech representations and dependencies are obtained by the self-attention mechanism across the entire sequence of latent representations end-to-end. In (Conneau et al., 2021), multilingual pre-training of Wav2Vec2.0 model on 53 languages with more than 56k hours of unlabeled speech data (*XLSR-53*) has shown to construct better speech representations for cross-lingual transfer. It is in this context that we consider fine-tuning this model on creole languages. In (Evain et al., 2021), several Wav2Vec2.0 models (*LeBenchmark*) specific to French language were pretrained. We propose to fine-tune these models on creole languages. Results are generated with a Connectionist Temporal Classification (CTC) beam search decoder (Graves et al., 2006). CTC is an algorithm that assign a probability for any Y given an X. In our case X represent the acoustic features generated by *LeBenchmark* and Y the items in the orthographic transcription. The combination of *LeBenchmark* and CTC allowed us to produce an orthographic transcription of every speech segment provided by the VAD algorithm.

3.4 Evaluation

A gold standard has been created by the second author using the transcription automatically generated. We computed a Character Error Rate (CER) and a Word Error Rate (WER) on a set of 549 utterances. WER and CER calculates the percentage of items (words or character) that are incorrectly recognised in relation to the total number of items in a reference transcript. We obtained a CER of 0.45 and a WER of 0.728. We present in figure 1 the distribution of the WER and CER per utterances. To improve the visibility of the figure, We removed 5 examples that were too high. Although the overall results may be deemed suboptimal, the boxplot analysis reveals that a considerable proportion of utterances exhibit a WER of less than 50%. This suggests that a significant number of the generated utterances remain usable for downstream applications.

While evaluating a speech recognition system, its usability is often only based on the WER and CER . The results obtained are not groundbreaking but our collaboration between NLP scientists and linguists could help us understand how the system created is useful, how it can be exploited and how it can be improved.

Code-mixing: An under-resourced language is generally in contact with a widely spoken language. In our case, because French is the official language of Guadeloupe island and because some of the linguists involved in the data collection were English speakers, Gwadloupéyen, French and English were intertwined in the recordings. Non-Gwadloupéyen segments were then transcribed with the Gwadloupéyen norms. It seems unlikely to automatically differentiate French and Gwadloupéyen segments due to their lexical similarity. However, recent language diarisation tool could help us to filter out English segments (e.g. Liu et al., 2021).

Voice Activity Detection: VAD was highly accurate and saved time by filtering out non-speech segments. A few inaccuracies have however been mentioned specifically for segments starting with non-voiced consonants. the algorithm also tended to over-segment some segments that belonged together.

Automatic transcription: The quality of the transcriptions generated was not uniform across the recording (cf. Figure 1). While some transcriptions were not exploitable at all, others happen to be helpful support for transcription. On one hand, some of the utterance had a WER closed to 0 which allowed us to just copy paste the generated transcription to the gold standard with minor corrections. On the other, for utterances with more errors, the transcription could help to more clearly identify what is said.

Transcription errors: Besides the errors due to code mixing, most of the errors of the systems were due to oversegmentation of tokens. However, this type of errors could be mitigated by plugging a language model at the end of the CTC system. Another error noticed was the difficulty of the system to correctly identify the nasals which are usually recognised as orals (cf. Table 1).

4 Conclusion

We have detailed the first stage of a joint effort between field linguists and NLP experts to aid in transcribing Kréyòl Gwadloupéyen field linguistic data. Our approach involved using a voice ac-

comments	gold standard	automatic generation
the final nasal is recognised as two orals	zot matinike gwadloupeyen	zoln patinike gwadloup ee
the sentence was French	deux saison	deu sezon
segmentation error	zo kay an grante	jo kay angrandte
segmentation errors and nasal confusion	matinik e gwadloupeyen	martini ke gwadelou pe ent
segmentation error	se limajiner a sa	se limaj jener a sa
segmentation and transcription errors	byen pale de bonda nou kay soukre bonda	mye fame de gonda nou ka ai soucebo

Table 1: Examples of transcriptions

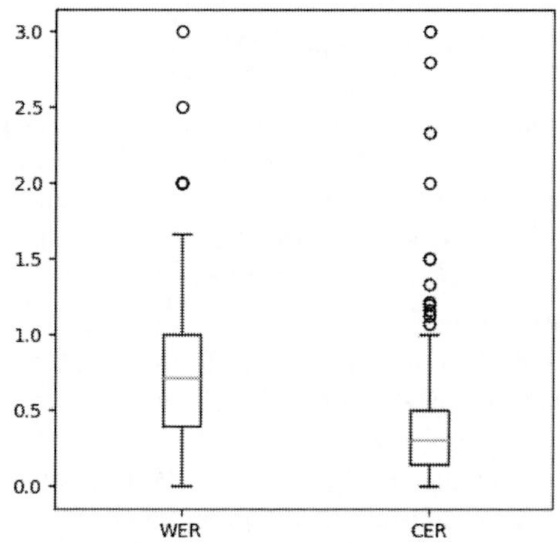

Figure 1: WER and CER distributions

tivity detection system combined with a wav2vec and CTC-based speech recognition model to transcribe raw recordings. The automatically generated transcription was then utilised to establish a gold standard.

Our initial work has prompted us to consider possibilities beyond conventional metrics such as WER and CER and to explore how even a transcription with a high error rate can still be useful. These early results have led us to question the relevance of standard metrics for evaluating a transcription system that can output words out of vocabulary. While a naive approach would be to assume that an automatically generated transcription is simply a starting point for post-editing and corrections (Bird, 2020, p.2), we have found that it can offer support for creating a gold standard and help transcribers better identify the content of a recording, especially when they are not confident in the target language. Moreover, the errors made by the system have increased our understanding of the requirements for a speech recognition system, potentially leading to improved recording quality in the future.

Moving forward, we will look to improve the output of the system. This will involve utilising an overlapping speech detector to eliminate noisy utterances, employing a language model to prevent token hyper-segmentation, and gradually improving the quality of the training data to enhance the transcription.

References

Oliver Adams, Benjamin Galliot, Guillaume Wisniewski, Nicholas Lambourne, Ben Foley, Rahasya Sanders-Dwyer, Janet Wiles, Alexis Michaud, Séverine Guillaume, Laurent Besacier, et al. 2021. User-friendly automatic transcription of low-resource languages: Plugging ESPnet into ELPIS. In *ComputEL-4: Fourth Workshop on the Use of Computational Methods in the Study of Endangered Languages*.

Alexei Baevski, Michael Auli, and Abdelrahman Mohamed. 2019. Effectiveness of self-supervised pre-training for speech recognition. *arXiv preprint arXiv:1911.03912*.

Alexei Baevski, Yuhao Zhou, Abdelrahman Mohamed, and Michael Auli. 2020. wav2vec 2.0: A framework for self-supervised learning of speech representations. *Advances in Neural Information Processing Systems*, 33:12449–12460.

Mat Bettinson and Steven Bird. 2017. Developing a suite of mobile applications for collaborative language documentation. In *2nd Workshop on Computational Methods for Endangered Languages*, pages 156–164.

Steven Bird. 2020. Sparse transcription. *Computational Linguistics*, 46(4):713–744.

Steven Bird, Florian Hanke, Oliver Adams, and Haejoong Lee. 2014. Aikuma: A mobile app for collaborative language documentation. In *Proceedings of the Workshop on the Use of Computational Methods in the Study of Endangered Languages*, pages 1–5. ACL.

Paul Boersma and David Weenink. 1996. Praat, a system for doing phonetics by computer, version 3.4. *Institute of Phonetic sciences of the University of Amsterdam, Report*, 132:182.

Robert Chaudenson. 2004. La créolisation: théorie, applications, implications. *La créolisation*, pages 1–480.

Alexis Conneau, Alexei Baevski, Ronan Collobert, Abdelrahman Mohamed, and Michael Auli. 2021. Unsupervised cross-lingual representation learning for speech recognition. *Proceedings of Interspeech 2021*.

Solène Evain, Ha Nguyen, Hang Le, Marcely Zanon Boito, Salima Mdhaffar, Sina Alisamir, Ziyi Tong, Natalia Tomashenko, Marco Dinarelli, Titouan Parcollet, Alexandre Allauzen, Yannick Estève, Benjamin Lecouteux, François Portet, Solange Rossato, Fabien Ringeval, Didier Schwab, and Laurent Besacier. 2021. LeBenchmark: A Reproducible Framework for Assessing Self-Supervised Representation Learning from Speech. In *Proc. Interspeech 2021*, pages 1439–1443.

Ben Foley, Joshua T Arnold, Rolando Coto-Solano, Gautier Durantin, T Mark Ellison, Daan van Esch, Scott Heath, Frantisek Kratochvil, Zara Maxwell-Smith, David Nash, et al. 2018. Building speech recognition systems for language documentation: The CoEDL Endangered Language Pipeline and Inference System (ELPIS). In *Proceedings of The 6th International Workshop on Spoken Language Technologies for Under-Resourced Languages*, pages 205–209.

Elodie Gauthier. 2018. *Collecter Transcrire Analyser: quand la machine assiste le linguiste dans son travail de terrain*. Ph.D. thesis, Université Grenoble Alpes.

Elodie Gauthier, David Blachon, Laurent Besacier, Guy-Noël Kouarata, Martine Adda-Decker, Annie Rialland, Gilles Adda, and Grégoire Bachman. 2016. LIG-Aikuma: A mobile app to collect parallel speech for under-resourced language studies. *Interspeech 2016*, pages 381–382.

Luke Gessler. 2022. Closing the NLP gap documentary linguistics and NLP need a shared software infrastructure. In *Proceedings of the 5th Workshop on the Use of Computational Methods in the Study of Endangered Languages*, pages 119–126.

Alex Graves, Santiago Fernández, Faustino Gomez, and Jürgen Schmidhuber. 2006. Connectionist temporal classification: labelling unsegmented sequence data with recurrent neural networks. In *Proceedings of the 23rd international conference on Machine learning*, pages 369–376.

Vishwa Gupta and Gilles Boulianne. 2020a. Automatic transcription challenges for Inuktitut, a low-resource polysynthetic language. In *Proceedings of the 12th Language Resources and Evaluation Conference (LREC)*, pages 2521–27.

Vishwa Gupta and Gilles Boulianne. 2020b. Speech transcription challenges for resource constrained Indigenous language Cree. In *Proceedings of the 1st Joint Workshop on Spoken Language Technologies for Under-Resourced Languages and Collaboration and Computing for Under-Resourced Languages (CCURL)*, pages 362–367.

Nikolaus P. Himmelmann. 1998. *Documentary and descriptive linguistics*, volume 36. de Gruyter.

Béatrice Jeannot-Fourcaud and Paulette Durizot Jno-Baptiste. 2008. L'enseignement du français en contexte diglossique Guadeloupéen: état des lieux et propositions. *Former les enseignants du XXIème siècle dans toute la francophonie*, pages 61–73.

Kazuya Kawakami, Luyu Wang, Chris Dyer, Phil Blunsom, and Aaron van den Oord. 2020. Learning robust and multilingual speech representations. In *Findings of the Association for Computational Linguistics: EMNLP 2020*, pages 1182–1192, Online. Association for Computational Linguistics.

William Lane, Mat Bettinson, and Steven Bird. 2021. A computational model for interactive transcription. In *Proceedings of the 2nd Workshop on Data Science with Human in the Loop: Language Advances*, pages 105–111.

Éric Le Ferrand, Steven Bird, and Laurent Besacier. 2022. Fashioning local designs from generic speech technologies in an Australian Aboriginal community. In *Proceedings of the 29th International Conference on Computational Linguistics*, pages 4274–4285.

Hexin Liu, Leibny Paola García Perera, Xinyi Zhang, Justin Dauwels, Andy W.H. Khong, Sanjeev Khudanpur, and Suzy J. Styles. 2021. End-to-End Language Diarization for Bilingual Code-Switching Speech. In *Proc. Interspeech 2021*, pages 1489–1493.

Cécile Macaire, Didier Schwab, Benjamin Lecouteux, and Emmanuel Schang. 2022. Automatic speech recognition and query by example for creole languages documentation. In *Findings of the Association for Computational Linguistics: ACL 2022*, pages 2512–2520.

Sarah Ruth Moeller. 2014. SayMore, a tool for language documentation productivity. *Language Documentation and Conservation*, 8:66–74.

Salikoko S Mufwene. 1997. Jargons, pidgins, creoles, and koines: What are they? *CREOLE LANGUAGE LIBRARY*, 19:35–70.

Lambert-Félix Prudent. 1999. Des baragouins à la langue antillaise. *Des Baragouins à la langue Antillaise*, pages 1–214.

Jiatong Shi, Jonathan D Amith, Rey Castillo García, Esteban Guadalupe Sierra, Kevin Duh, and Shinji Watanabe. 2021. Leveraging end-to-end asr for endangered language documentation: An empirical study on Yolóxochitl Mixtec. In *Proceedings of the 16th Conference of the European Chapter of the Association for Computational Linguistics: Main Volume*, pages 1134–1145.

Viveka Velupillai. 2015. Pidgins, creoles and mixed languages. *Pidgins, Creoles and Mixed Languages*, pages 1–626.

Peter Wittenburg, Hennie Brugman, Albert Russel, Alex Klassmann, and Han Sloetjes. 2006. ELAN: a professional framework for multimodality research. In *5th International Conference on Language Resources and Evaluation*, pages 1556–15.

Unsupervised part-of-speech induction for language description: Modeling documentation materials in Kolyma Yukaghir

Albert Ventayol-Boada and **Nathan Roll** and **Simon Todd**
University of California, Santa Barbara
{aventayolboada, nroll, sjtodd}@ucsb.edu

Abstract

This study investigates the clustering of words into Part-of-Speech (POS) classes in Kolyma Yukaghir. In grammatical descriptions, lexical items are assigned to POS classes based on their morphological paradigms. Discursively, however, these classes share a fair amount of morphology. In this study, we turn to POS induction to evaluate if classes based on quantification of the distributions in which roots and affixes are used can be useful for language description purposes, and, if so, what those classes might be. We qualitatively compare clusters of roots and affixes based on four different definitions of their distributions. The results show that clustering is more reliable for words that typically bear more morphology. Additionally, the results suggest that the number of POS classes in Kolyma Yukaghir might be smaller than stated in current descriptions. This study thus demonstrates how unsupervised learning methods can provide insights for language description, particularly for highly inflectional languages.

1 Introduction

Many NLP applications and linguistic investigations are facilitated by having Part-of-Speech (POS) tags for words in context. Providing such tags flexibly and at scale for novel texts requires a POS tagger. When working with low-resource languages, it is often infeasibly labor-intensive to develop labeled data that would enable the training of a supervised tagger, or even to develop a lexicon that delimits the set of tags that may be appropriate for each word (Hasan and Ng, 2009) and thereby facilitates the training of an accurate unsupervised tagger (e.g. Goldwater and Griffiths, 2007). Working with such languages requires turning to POS *induction*, which clusters words according to the contexts in which they occur in an unannotated corpus. Following the *distributional hypothesis* (Harris, 1951, 1954), words that occur in similar contexts are assumed to belong to the same POS class.

POS induction is a potentially useful tool for the documentary linguist. However, its utility for endangered and underdocumented languages remains to be established, as it is not always clear what the POS class of a word should be in many such languages or even whether the notion of POS classes as established for high-resource European languages is appropriate (Bender, 2011; Finn et al., 2022), due to potentially high degrees of polyfunctionality (Mithun, 2017; Hieber, 2021; Carter, 2023). The goal of this paper is to evaluate the insights of POS induction for language documentation, through a case study on Kolyma Yukaghir (Yukaghiric), a highly inflectional endangered language of Northeastern Siberia (Republic of Sakha, Russia).

2 POS induction in highly inflectional languages

POS induction leverages distributional information by representing each word as a *co-occurrence vector*, which reflects how often it appears near each other word in a corpus, and clustering words with similar vectors. This approach is successful for languages that display fairly rigid word order and little inflection, like English, because the vectors are characterized by frequent function words that predominantly co-occur with words in certain POS classes, such as "the" and "to". However, it is not so successful for highly inflectional languages, in which the corresponding function elements are bound morphemes (Dasgupta and Ng, 2007; Bender, 2011).

Successful unsupervised POS induction for highly inflectional languages requires building morphological information into the model. This approach leverages the fact that inflectional affixes are strongly associated with POS classes. If the POS classes of the affixes in a word are known, they can be used to delimit the set of possible POS classes for the root of that word (Hajič, 2000; Duh and Kirchhoff, 2006). If the POS classes of affixes are not known, the distributional hypothesis can be applied

Proceedings of the Second Workshop on NLP Applications to Field Linguistics, pages 23–29
May 6, 2023 ©2023 Association for Computational Linguistics

at the morphological level: roots that have similar distributions of co-occurrence with affixes can be assumed to belong to the same POS class (Cucerzan and Yarowsky, 2000; Clark, 2003; Freitag, 2004; Dasgupta and Ng, 2007).

However, building morphological information into POS induction may not be successful in all languages. There may be three major issues, which we illustrate with examples from Kolyma Yukaghir.

The first issue is that the same affix may attach to roots that would traditionally be considered to have distinct POS classes, and as a result are analyzed as homonyms. In our examples, the suffix *-n* attaches to nouns when they modify a noun (1) or encode the arguments of a postposition (2), in which case it is glossed as "genitive". An identical morpheme attaches to numerals (3) and "adjectives" (4), but in these cases it is often glossed as "attributive" or "adverbializer", respectively.

(1) *одун мархиль,*
odu-**n** marqil',
Yukaghir-**GEN** girl
'(The) Yukaghir girl' ("Yearly meetings")

(2) *таа нумөн ниӈиэлгэн*
taa numö-**n** niŋeel-gən
there house-**GEN** between-PROL
эйрэт,
ej-rə-t,
walk-NONIT-CVB.CTX
'Walking along the houses there' ("Tobacco")

(3) *иркин йалҕилгэ йахайэ,*
irk-i-**n** jalğil-gə jaqa-jə,
one-EP-**ATTR** lake-LOC reach-1SG
'I arrived at a lake' ("Tobacco")

(4) *чомоон йукоодьоон оодьэ,*
čom-oo-**n** juk-oo-d'oon oo-d'ə,
big-RES-**ADVZ** small-RES-NMLZ be-1SG
'I was very small'
[Lit. 'I was smalling greatly'] ("Tobacco")

This issue reflects a problem with traditional considerations: labels like "genitive", "attributive" or "adverbializer" reflect a view that tries to bend Kolyma Yukaghir to ill-fitting POS classes developed for other (European) languages. It is more fitting to characterize the grammatical relations in the language's own terms (Mithun, 2001; Epps, 2011). From this perspective, examples (1–4) display a single form that attaches to a modifier to grammatically mark its relationship with the modified. That relationship may be of a more attributive nature like in (1) or (3), but it may also be of another kind, as in (2) and (4).

The second issue is that the same root may appear with affixes that are prototypically associated with traditionally distinct POS classes (Maslova, 2003). Numerals and "adjectives" appear in (3–4) with a suffix that is indistinguishable from prototypically nominal case-marking in (1–2), but they are also attested as the main predication of a clause bearing prototypical verbal morphology, such as aspect, evidentiality, person and number (5–6).

(5) *иркидьэ мит йаал**ооиили***
irk-i-d'ə mit jaa-l-**oo-iili**
one-EP-PTCP 1PL three-EP-**RES-1PL**
'Once we were three'
[Lit. 'Once we threed'] ("The first lesson")

(6) *киндьэ,*
kind'ə
moon
'(The) moon'

*иилэмэдэ чом**мунульэл**,*
iilə-mə-də čom-**mu-nu-l'əl-0**
other-TEMP-UNK big-**IMPF-INCH-EV-3SG**
'Sometimes the moon becomes big'
[Lit. 'Sometimes the moon bigs'] ("The first lesson")

The third issue, which is a consequence of the first two, is that two roots may have highly similar affix co-occurrence distributions but nevertheless be considered as having distinct POS classes. Despite the similarities between numerals and "adjectives" in the examples (3-6), they are treated differently in grammars: "adjectives" are grouped with verbs (Krejnovič, 1982; Maslova, 2003; Nagasaki, 2010), while numerals are either considered as a separate POS class (Maslova, 2003) or classified simultaneously with adnominals and verbs (Nagasaki, 2010). These differences in conceptualization result in a different number of POS classes: 8 according to Maslova (2003), and 6 to Nagasaki (2010).

The large degree of shared morphology across roots in such highly inflectional languages raises the question of whether applying the distributional hypothesis at the morphological level is appropriate, as well as the question of what the relevant POS classes might be in such languages in the first place. We explore these questions from a bottom-up, data-driven approach, with a case study on Kolyma Yukaghir. Specifically, we seek to identify and evaluate the number of POS clusters through unsupervised induction, without specifying a predetermined value.

3 Kolyma Yukaghir

Like other languages in the Siberian linguistic area (Anderson, 2006; Pakendorf, 2010), Kolyma Yukaghir is strongly head-final, and it displays SV/AOV constituent order with nominative-accusative alignment. Morphologically, Kolyma Yukaghir is a predominantly agglutinating, suffix-dominant language, with partially fusional morphology. Suffixes display some allomorphy due to residual vowel harmony and consonantal assimilation processes (Krejnovič, 1982; Maslova, 2003; Nagasaki, 2010).

In terms of morphological complexity, roots show differences in terms of the number and range of affixes they typically occur with. Roots used "verbally" (i.e., for predication) have the largest number of affixal slots, some of which can be filled by a wide range of possible items (e.g., aspect). Roots used "nominally" have fewer slots, which can typically be filled by fewer possible affixes, and sometimes occur without affixes at all (e.g., *kind'ə* in 6).

In this study, we analyzed 19 of the 40 monologic texts collected in the late 20th century (Nikolaeva and Mayer, 2004). These texts were narrated by five different speakers in the community and include a variety of genres: folktales, personal and fantastical stories, descriptions of games and competitions, an account of fortune telling, etc.

To prepare the data, we stripped the texts of glosses, transliterated them into Cyrillic orthography, and divided them into intonation units (IU; Chafe, 1979, 1992). IUs are defined as "a stretch of speech uttered under a single coherent intonation contour" (Du Bois et al., 1993:47) or the "spurts of language" in which speakers typically produce speech (Chafe, 1994:29). Affix boundary markers from the original transcriptions were maintained, so the choice of writing system did not impact the results. However, we removed root-internal boundary markers in compounds (13 words total). We also removed clitic boundary markers, replacing them with white space in the case of proclitics, and affix boundary markers in the case of enclitics. This treatment yielded texts that follow established written conventions as closely as possible. Additionally, it meant that every word presented the same structure: if one or more morphological boundaries were present, the left-most morpheme was the root, and any subsequent elements were suffixes.

After preprocessing, the data contained 3,513 word tokens (where a token was taken to be anything bounded by white space). These word tokens contained 3,513 root tokens of 663 types and 3,911 affix tokens of 138 types.

Definition	Example
ROOT(ROOTS; IU)	irk-*i-d'ə* mit **jaa**-*l-oo-iili*
ROOT(AFFIXES; WORD)	*irk-i-d'ə mit* **jaa**-l-oo-iili
AFFIX(ROOTS; WORD)	*irk-i-d'ə mit* jaa-*l-oo*-**iili**
AFFIX(AFFIXES; WORD)	*irk-i-d'ə mit* *jaa*-l-oo-**iili**

Table 1: Examples of co-occurrence vector definitions, based on (5). The vector for the target (bold) includes the counts of each underlined item in the box, summed across all occurrences of the target in the corpus.

4 Methods

We obtained co-occurrence vectors for roots and affixes under four distinct definitions. The first definition, ROOT(ROOTS; IU), yielded a vector for each root, based on the roots it co-occurs with in an IU, as shown in the first row of Table 1 based on example (5). We constructed a sparse matrix that counted how often each root in the corpus occurred in the same IU as each other root, as well as how often it occurred alone within an IU.

We removed rows corresponding to roots that only ever occurred alone within an IU, then applied truncated SVD to obtain a dense matrix with 40 columns, from which we extracted the rows. We obtained co-occurrence vectors by normalizing these rows to have unit length.

We obtained vectors similarly for the remaining three definitions: ROOT(AFFIXES; WORD) yielded a vector for each root, based on the affixes that attach to it; AFFIX(ROOTS; WORD) yielded a vector for each affix, based on the roots it attaches to; and AFFIX(AFFIXES; WORD) yielded a vector for each affix, based on the affixes it co-occurs with in a word. Examples of these definitions are shown in Table 1. For ROOT(AFFIXES; WORD) and AFFIX(AFFIXES; WORD), our vectors also included counts for the number of times a root occurred without any attached affixes and the number of times an affix was the only affix attached to a word, respectively.

For each definition, we first removed elements that only ever occurred as isolates in the corpus (for ROOT(ROOTS; IU), roots that only ever occurred alone in an IU; for ROOT(AFFIXES; WORD), roots that only ever occurred without affixes; and for AFFIX(AFFIXES; WORD), affixes that never occurred alongside other affixes in a word). We then used k-means clustering on the vectors of remaining elements under each definition to induce classes of roots/affixes that have similar distributions within the corpus. We picked the number of clusters using the elbow method, where cluster quality was measured by inertia. For qualitative interpretation, we identified the 20 roots/affixes with the highest degree of centrality from each cluster.

These four definitions represent different ways to approach POS induction. ROOT(ROOTS; IU) and ROOT(AFFIXES; WORD) assign each root to a class, as is typical for POS in European languages. We expect ROOT(AFFIXES; WORD) to be better than ROOT(ROOTS; IU) for Kolyma Yukaghir because it incorporates crucial morphological information; however, we do not expect it to be particularly useful, due to the large degree of shared morphology across roots. AFFIX(ROOTS; WORD) and AFFIX(AFFIXES; WORD) assign each affix to a class, which allows the POS of a root to be determined in context by the affixes that are attached to it. We expect these definitions to be more useful than the root-wise ones because they reflect the polyfunctional nature of the language. Given the potential that affixes may mark different functional roles in Kolyma Yukaghir than is typically assumed for European languages, and may therefore co-occur with each other broadly, we might expect AFFIX(AFFIXES; WORD) to be less useful than AFFIX(ROOTS; WORD); however, the utility of AFFIX(ROOTS; WORD) ultimately depends on the extent to which roots have (gradient) prototypical associations with traditional POS roles.

5 Results

As shown in Figure 1, the elbow method identified 2 clusters (of non-isolates) for 3 definitions, and 3 clusters for ROOT(AFFIXES; WORD). Figure 2 visualizes the clusters under each definition using t-SNE.

The qualitative analysis of the 20 words with the highest degree of centrality under ROOT(ROOTS; IU) shows a lot of variability. Words closest to the center in the small cluster ($n = 55$) include Russian adverb loanwords (e.g., 'later'), pronouns (e.g., 'y'all', 'who'), nouns (e.g., 'hoof'), verbs (e.g., 'blow') and "adjectives" (e.g., 'fast'). Similarly, the big cluster ($n = 192$) does not display a clear thread; we find the same categories as above.

The clusters under ROOT(AFFIXES; WORD) show more consistency, as expected. The 20 words in the smallest cluster ($n = 116$) are almost exclusively nominal roots (e.g., 'river'), with the exception of

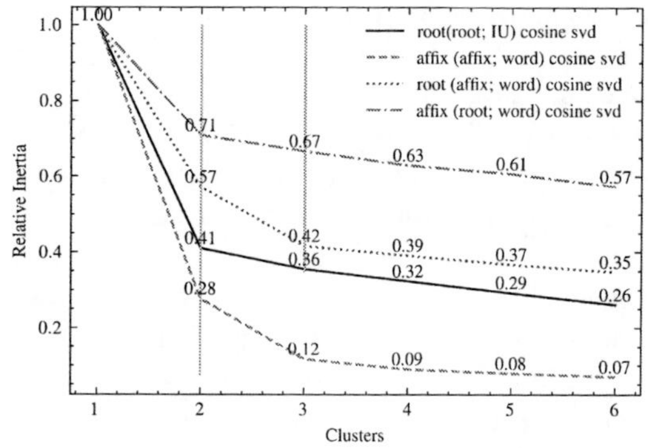

Figure 1: Number of clusters identified by the elbow method

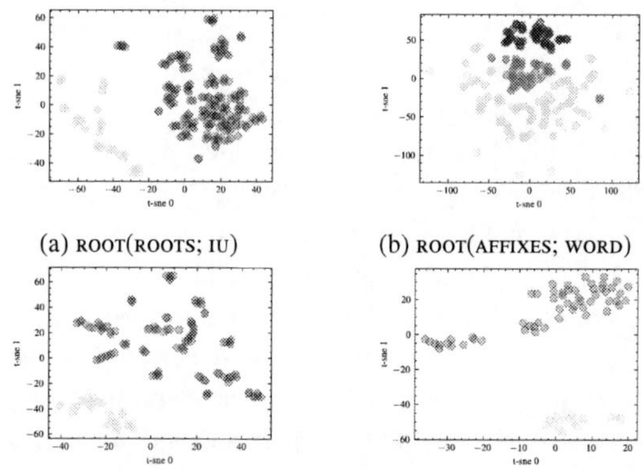

(a) ROOT(ROOTS; IU)

(b) ROOT(AFFIXES; WORD)

(c) AFFIX(ROOTS; WORD)

(d) AFFIX(AFFIXES; WORD)

Figure 2: k-means clusters under the 4 definitions

the two copulas (of which one also functions as a placeholder), one verbal root (e.g., '(be) outside') and a homonym (e.g., *aŭuu-* 'shoot', 'only'). We find the opposite pattern in the slightly bigger cluster ($n = 123$), where all the roots are more verbal in nature (e.g., 'hear') but one (e.g., 'bell'). The third and biggest cluster ($n = 249$) displays some variability; we find nominal (e.g., 'old woman') and verbal roots (e.g., 'take'), along with "adjectives" (e.g., 'good'), pronouns (e.g., 'what'), and nouns that can function as postpositions (e.g., 'back').

As for the clusters of affixes, AFFIX(AFFIXES; WORD) yields similar behavior to ROOT(ROOTS; IU) with a very asymmetric split. All the affixes in the small cluster ($n = 16$) are verbal, and the 20 affixes returned for the big cluster ($n = 56$) are also predominantly verbal, with the exception of a plural and a genitive/attributive allomorph.

The results for AFFIX(ROOTS; WORD) are more insightful, as expected. All but 3 of the 20 affixes in the big cluster ($n = 102$) mark verbal functions (e.g., inchoative); the exceptions are two case markers and the directional -ӈудэ. In the small cluster ($n = 36$), two thirds of the affixes returned were nominal (e.g. 3rd person possessive), whereas the remaining third were verbal and predominantly associated with non-finiteness.

6 Discussion & Conclusion

The number of clusters identified by the elbow method is rather small. This could be because there is not enough data to make finer distinctions in the clustering process, beyond a coarse split into prototypically "nominal" and "verbal" POS classes (and a third mixed class in ROOT(AFFIXES; WORD)). Alternatively, it could be because Kolyma Yukaghir permits a given affix (or, to some extent, root) to be used in myriad ways, such that the treatment of each root/affix as monolithic (in terms of representing one feature in the vectors, and in terms of having only one POS class) obscures deeper complexity.

As for the qualitative analysis of the clusters, the results suggest that ROOT(AFFIXES; WORD) indeed offers a more informative clustering than ROOT(ROOTS; IU). The latter definition fails to find structure in the data, whereas the former returns two cohesive clusters (with a nominal and a verbal tendency) and a third cluster with some variability. This variability, however, reflects in part the polyfunctional nature of the language. Some roots that look prototypically nominal, like 'old woman', can bear verbal morphology to convey predicative possession (i.e., 'have a wife'), and thus their clustering with "adjectives", like 'good', that can also be marked with nominal and verbal morphology is coherent with their distributions. Overall, the smaller number of function words makes the incorporation of morphological information particularly useful as anticipated.

As for affixes, the clustering under AFFIX(AFFIXES; WORD) is less useful than that under AFFIX(ROOTS; WORD). These results suggest that, to a certain degree, some roots might be prototypically associated with noun and verb POS roles. In addition, the homogeneity of the bigger cluster in AFFIX(ROOTS; WORD) with verbal functions indicates that verbal affixes might be a more reliable source of information. This probably results from finite, assertion-making words being more morphologically complex: a "verbal" root can carry several affixes simultaneously – marking it for tense, aspect, evidentiality, and person/number – whereas "nominal" roots tend not to carry many affixes at once. Nominal stems can be marked for possession, case, and evaluatives, but rarely do all co-occur. Thus, our removal of isolates – affixes that never occurred alongside other affixes in a word – is likely to have affected nominal affixes more than verbal affixes.

Taken together, the results suggest that applying the distributional hypothesis at the morphological level in a context with significant shared morphology can yield successful results, especially when clustering roots and affixes each on the basis of the other. Clustering might be more reliable for words that typically bear more morphology. However, the results can be fairly coarse-grained; to obtain finer-grained insights, more data and/or a more complex (mixture-based) approach may be necessary.

Additionally, the results also provide some insight into what the relevant POS classes in Kolyma Yukaghir might be. Rather than the eight and six POS classes listed in grammatical descriptions (Maslova, 2003 and Nagasaki, 2010, respectively), the clustering suggests a binary split at the morphological level centering around nominal and verbal functions, with the possibility of a third mixed class. Further research is needed to investigate the degree to which this third distinction is categorical or represents a cline with nouns and verbs on opposite ends.

Limitations

An important aspect of this study is the use of spoken data for the analysis, which might have had some effect on the results for ROOT(ROOTS; IU). The average IU length is 2.06 words, which effectively removes one neighbor for this definition.

Similarly, it is possible the different text genres may present different frequencies of words and constructions, which would influence the distributions underpinning POS induction. Addressing the effect of genre for POS induction is beyond the scope of this paper and remains an issue for future research.

In addition, we used morphologically segmented data rather than unsegmented data, which other POS induction studies use. Using morphologically segmented words requires some pre-existing knowledge and understanding of word structure and morphological paradigms in the language.

Finally, we treated all suffixation equally, since signs of derivation are not always clear. For highly inflectional languages with productive derivation, our approach might need a different operationalization of distributional information.

Ethics Statement

This study stems from a wider project to collect various documentation materials for Kolyma Yukaghir, and its close relative Tundra Yukaghir, and standardize them in the practical orthographies to make them more accessible to community members. With these materials, different studies are being carried out using machine learning methods in order to deepen our understanding of the grammatical structure of the languages. Ultimately, the goal is to use this knowledge to support language revitalization initiatives under way in the community.

Additionally, in this article we refrain from engaging in a "numbers game" to characterize the context of language endangerment in the Yukaghir community, as numbers are not well equipped to describe, explain or contextualize the factors that cause processes of language shift (Dobrin et al., 2009; Moore et al., 2010; Davis, 2017).

Abbreviations

1	first person	LOC	locative
3	third person	NMLZ	nominalizer
ADVZ	adverbializer	NONIT	noniterative
ATTR	attributive	PL	plural
CTX	contextual	PROL	prolative
CVB	converb	PTCP	participle
EP	epenthesis	RES	resultative
EV	evidential	SG	singular
GEN	genitive	TEMP	temporal
IMPF	imperfective	UNK	unknown/unclear
INCH	inchoative		

References

Gregory D.S. Anderson. 2006. Towards a typology of the Siberian linguistic area. In Yaron Matras, April McMahon, and Nigel Vincent, editors, *Linguistic Areas: Convergence in Historical and Typological Perspective*, pages 266–300. Palgrave Macmillan, London.

Emily M. Bender. 2011. On Achieving and Evaluating Language-Independence in NLP. *Linguistic Issues in Language Technology*, 6(3):1–26.

Matthew Carter. 2023. Polyfunctional argument markers in Ket: Implicative structure within the word. *Morphology*.

Wallace L. Chafe. 1979. The Flow of Thought and the Flow of Language. In Talmy Givón, editor, *Discourse and Syntax*, pages 159–181. Brill, New York.

Wallace L. Chafe. 1992. Intonation Units and prominences in English natural discourse. In *Proceedings of the IRCS Workshop on Prosody in Natural Speech*, pages 41–52, Philadelphia. University of Pennsylvania Press.

Wallace L. Chafe. 1994. *Discourse, Consciousness, and Time*. The University of Chicago Press, Chicago, London.

Alexander Clark. 2003. Combining distributional and morphological information for part of speech induction. In *Proceedings of the 10th Conference of the European Chapter of the Association for Computational Linguistics*, pages 59–66, Budapest, Hungary. Association for Computational Linguistics.

Silviu Cucerzan and David Yarowsky. 2000. Language Independent, Minimally Supervised Induction of Lexical Probabilities. In *Proceedings of the 38th Annual Meeting of the Association for Computational Linguistics*, pages 270–277, Hong Kong. Association for Computational Linguistics.

Sajib Dasgupta and Vincent Ng. 2007. Unsupervised part-of-speech acquisition for resource-scarce languages. In *Proceedings of the 2007 Joint Conference on Empirical Methods in Natural Language Processing and Computational Natural Language Learning*, pages 218–227, Prague, Czech Republic. Association for Computational Linguistics.

Jenny L. Davis. 2017. Resisting rhetorics of language endangerment: Reclamation through Indigenous language survivance. *Language Documentation and Description*, 14:37–58.

Lise M. Dobrin, Peter K. Austin, and David Nathan. 2009. Dying to be counted: the commodification of endangered languages in documentary linguistics. *Language Documentation and Description*, 6:37–52.

John W. Du Bois, Stephan Schuetze-Coburn, Susanna Cumming, and Danae Paolino. 1993. Outline of Discourse Transcription. In Jane A. Edwards and Martin D. Lampert, editors, *Talking data: Transcription and coding in discourse research*, pages 45–89. Lawrence Erlbaum Associates Publishers, Hillsdale.

Kevin Duh and Katrin Kirchhoff. 2006. Lexicon acquisition for dialectal Arabic using transductive learning. In *Proceedings of the 2006 Conference on Empirical Methods in Natural Language Processing*, pages 399–407, Sydney, Australia. Association for Computational Linguistics.

Patience Epps. 2011. Linguistic Typology and Language Documentation. In Jae Jung Song, editor, *The Oxford Handbook of Linguistic Typology*, pages 634–649. Oxford University Press, Oxford.

Aoife Finn, Peter-Lucas Jones, Keoni Mahelona, Suzanne Duncan, and Gianna Leoni. 2022. Developing a part-of-speech tagger for te reo Māori. In

Proceedings of the Fifth Workshop on the Use of Computational Methods in the Study of Endangered Languages, pages 93–98, Dublin, Ireland. Association for Computational Linguistics.

Dayne Freitag. 2004. Toward Unsupervised Whole-Corpus Tagging. In *Proceedings of the 20th international conference on Computational Linguistics*, pages 357–363, Morristown, United States. Association for Computational Linguistics.

Sharon Goldwater and Thomas L. Griffiths. 2007. A fully Bayesian approach to unsupervised part-of-speech tagging. In *Proceedings of the 45th Annual Meeting of the Association for Computational Linguistics*, pages 744–751, Prague, Czech Republic. Association for Computational Linguistics.

Jan Hajič. 2000. Morphological tagging: data vs. dictionaries. In *Proceedings of the 1st Meeting of the North American Chapter of the Association for Computational Linguistics*, pages 94–101, Seattle, United States. Association for Computational Linguistics.

Zellig S. Harris. 1951. *Structural linguistics*. The University of Chicago Press, Chicago, London.

Zellig S. Harris. 1954. Distributional Structure. *Word*, 10(2-3):146–162.

Kazi Saidul Hasan and Vincent Ng. 2009. Weakly supervised part-of-speech tagging for morphologically-rich, resource-scarce languages. In *Proceedings of the 2th Conference of the European Chapter of the Association for Computational Linguistics*, pages 363–371, Athens, Greece. Association for Computational Linguistics.

Daniel W. Hieber. 2021. *Lexical polyfunctionality in discourse: A quantitative corpus-based approach*. Phd dissertation, University of California, Santa Barbara.

Eruxim A. Krejnovič. 1982. *Issledovanija i materialy po jukagirskomu jazyku*. Akademia Nauk SSSR, Moscow.

Elena S. Maslova. 2003. *A Grammar of Kolyma Yukaghir*. Mouton de Gruyter, Berlin, New York.

Marianne Mithun. 2001. Who shapes the record: the speaker and the linguist. In Paul Newman and Martha Ratliff, editors, *Linguistic fieldwork*, pages 34–54. Cambridge University Press, Cambridge.

Marianne Mithun. 2017. Polycategoriality and zero derivation: Insights from Central Alaskan Yup'ik Eskimo. In Valentina Vapnarsky and Edy Veneziano, editors, *Lexical Polycategoriality. Cross-linguistic, cross-theoretical and language acquisition approaches*, pages 155–174. John Benjamins Publishing Company, Philadelphia.

Robert E. Moore, Sari Pietikäinen, and Jan Blommaert. 2010. Counting the losses: Numbers as the language of language endangerment. *Sociolinguistic Studies*, 4(1):1–26.

Iku Nagasaki. 2010. Kolyma Yukaghir. In Yasuhiro Yamakoshi, editor, *Grammatical Sketches from the Field*, pages 213–256. Research Institute for Languages and Cultures of Asia and Africa (ILCAA), Tokyo.

Irina Nikolaeva and Thomas Mayer. 2004. Online Documentation of Kolyma Yukaghir.

Brigitte Pakendorf. 2010. Contact and Siberian languages. In Raymond Hickey, editor, *The Handbook of Language Contact*, pages 714–737. Wiley-Blackwell, Oxford.

Speech Database (Speech-DB) – An on-line platform for recording, storing, validating, and searching spoken language data

Jolene Poulin and **Daniel Dacanay** and **Antti Arppe**
Alberta Language Technology Lab (ALTLab)
Department of Linguistics, University of Alberta
{jcpoulin, dacanay, arppe}@ualberta.ca
https://altlab.ualberta.ca

Abstract

The Speech Database (Speech-DB: URL: https://speech-db.altlab.app) is an online platform for language documentation, written and spoken language validation, and speech exploration; its code-base is available as open source. In its current state, Speech-DB has expanded to contain content for several Indigenous languages spoken in Western Canada, having started with audio for the dialect of Plains Cree spoken in Maskwacîs, Alberta, Canada. Currently, it is used primarily for validation and storage. It can be accessed by anyone with an internet connection in six levels of access rights. What follows is the rationale for the development of speech-DB, an exploration of its features, and a description of usage scenarios, as well as initial user feedback on the application.

1 Introduction

The Speech Database (Speech-DB: https://speech-db.altlab.app) is an online platform of spoken language data intended for use in the preservation and documentation of less-resourced languages. With dual function as a searchable database for transcribed and translated audio data and as a validation interface for editing spoken dictionary entries, it is available online for anyone to use, and it is easily adaptable for use in various language pairs.

While Speech-DB has been used to store spoken data for multiple Indigenous languages and their dialects spoken in Western Canada, here we exemplify its use in language documentation primarily for Plains Cree (*nêhiyawêwin*, iso: crk), an Algonquian language spoken throughout Western Canada, specifically the dialect spoken in Maskwacîs, Alberta (Canada). This paper will review the objectives of Speech-DB, both at the time it was developed as well as how they evolved, the current and future features of the service, the means by which it was developed, and some key technical features. Furthermore, we discuss how the Speech-DB differs from other, similar services available online, as well as describe the practical usage of Speech-DB through a selection of qualitative user evaluations.

2 Background

The origins of Speech-DB may be traced to an earlier language documentation project; namely, the *Spoken Dictionary of Maskwacîs Cree / nêhiyawêwi-pîkiskwêwina maskwacîsihk* (Littlechild et al., 2018; Arppe et al., 2022a,b). This joint endeavor between Miyo Wahkohtowin Education (now part of the Maskwacîs Education Schools Commission (MESC: https://maskwacised.ca) and the Alberta Language Technology Lab (ALTLab: https://altlab.ualberta.ca), sought to achieve three primary goals: 1) to record audio for all entries ($n = 8996$) in an existing dictionary, the *Maskwacîs Dictionary of Cree Words / Nêhiyaw Pîkiskwêwinisa* (Maskwachees Cultural College, 2009), as spoken by multiple native speakers from Maskwacîs, Alberta (Canada); 2) to fill lexical gaps in the content of this dictionary; and 3) to elicit and record example sentences for as many of these entries as possible (Reule, 2018) This project resulted in the accumulation of 341 approximately 2-hour recording sessions, each of which involved two-to-four fluent native speakers of Cree and at least one linguist. These sessions were recorded at intervals in Maskwacîs between June 2014 and May 2018, and ultimately resulted in the elicitation of 20,299 Cree words and sentences, with anywhere between one and several tens of pronunciation tokens of the same entry by one or more speakers. In 2019-2020, these recording sessions were annotated by undergraduate students to isolate the Cree vocabulary items therein and align them with the transcriptions and English translations provided in the field elicitation sheets.

Proceedings of the Second Workshop on NLP Applications to Field Linguistics, pages 30–39
May 6, 2023 ©2023 Association for Computational Linguistics

3 Objectives and their evolution

The original objective for the development of Speech-DB was to construct a centralized database for the Maskwacîs Cree audio entries (and their associated metadata) in a format that was easily accessible from other services, such as *itwêwina* (`https://itwewina.altlab.app`), an online, morphologically intelligent Plains Cree – English dictionary (Arppe et al., 2018, 2022c). The process of validating the recording quality, Cree transcriptions, English translations, and metadata (e.g. speaker ID codes) of the database's audio recordings was initially planned to take place in-person in Maskwacîs. However, when in-person activities became all but impossible in early 2020, a new approach was needed to enable this validation task to take place virtually. The Speech-DB was subsequently expanded to support this task.

In the planning and organization of the various subtasks within the validation work, we aimed to optimize the impact of, and minimize the time commitment for, our native speaker consultants, who (in Maskwacîs) were predominantly elderly individuals whose time was in high demand for various other language documentation and instruction tasks. Thus, we divided the validation tasks into activities which categorically required the participation of a native speaker of Cree and tasks which could be accomplished by a linguist knowledgeable in the language. Therefore, the native speakers (or 'Language Experts') would be categorically needed for 1) judging the accuracy of English translations for all the Cree entries in the database (and providing corrections to these), 2) judging the accuracy and naturalness of Cree sentences (word choice, word order), as well as 3) judging the quality of each individual spoken token, in particular their exemplariness. Consequently, the supporting linguists could undertake preparatory standardization work, such as 1) reviewing and fixing any apparent inconsistencies in the Cree transcriptions, which is coupled with 2) reviewing the linguistic analyses of the transcriptions (including the lemma, stem, and other lexical information). This workflow is described in detail in Section 5. In addition, given that there were roughly 150,000 individual unvalidated recording tokens at the beginning of the validation process, provisionally made available through *itwêwina*, we also made it possible for any person to flag recordings in Speech-DB that were in any respect problematic. (i.e. poor recording quality, unusual transcription or translation) for review by linguists or language experts.

As the validation process proceeded to take place online (both asynchronously and synchronously through teleconference with Cree elders and other speakers in Maskwacîs), new features were added to ease the workflow, in effect extending the use of Speech-DB to (new) language documentation. One such additional feature was the ability to record entries directly into the Speech-DB. Previously, recordings had to be done on a separate computer or with a separate software, annotated by a linguist to segment relevant snippets from larger recordings, and then uploaded to the Speech-DB using a custom script written by the software developer. With the addition of this feature, any authorized user (see Section 4.1) can add a new recording directly to the Speech-DB, so long as they know the transcription and translation of the entry. These recordings are then subject to review and approval by a linguist prior to being made available to the general public.

The database is also structured in such a way that new language groups can be added with minimal technical effort. All that is required for the addition of a new language on Speech-DB is for the site administrator to enter in the new language family; users can then immediately begin adding and viewing entries. This new language family is then presented on the introductory page as a new section of the Speech-DB. New sections can be instantiated with no recordings as an empty version of the Speech-DB; with recordings supplied by a linguist or community member in a format that can be parsed and uploaded by the software developer.

Alternatively, sections containing only prompts for future recordings can be created. In the case of the last option, these prompts may be taken from handwritten, gestalt lists of entries, or, more effectively, from an existing, codified semantic domain set, such as that used in the SIL Rapid Word Collection Method (Boerger and Stutzman, 2018), which would both provide an overall structure for entries and ensure a relatively balanced coverage of the lexicon. Consequently, besides audio for Plains Cree spoken in Maskwacîs, Speech-DB has expanded to incorporate content for another Cree dialect spoken in *môswacîhk*, Saskatchewan, as well as selected outputs from a Plains Cree synthesizer (Harrigan et al., 2019). Additionally, extensive audio exists for the Dene language Tsuut'ina, imported into Speech-DB, as well as for three areal variants of the Siouan language Nakoda.

Speech-DB's search functionality was initially very basic, featuring only the option to search for entries matching a search string. However, as needs evolved, an advanced search feature was added, allowing users to search by a variety of attributes, including recording quality ('GOOD' or 'BAD'), speaker, morphological analysis, transcription, translation, and semantic classification. The last of these attributes, semantic classification, is based on the semantic domain assigned to the entry according to the aforementioned SIL Rapid Word Collection Methodology, which was used in the initial recordings sessions to collate similar vocabulary to be covered per each session. However, this semantic classification search functionality is not yet fully operational.

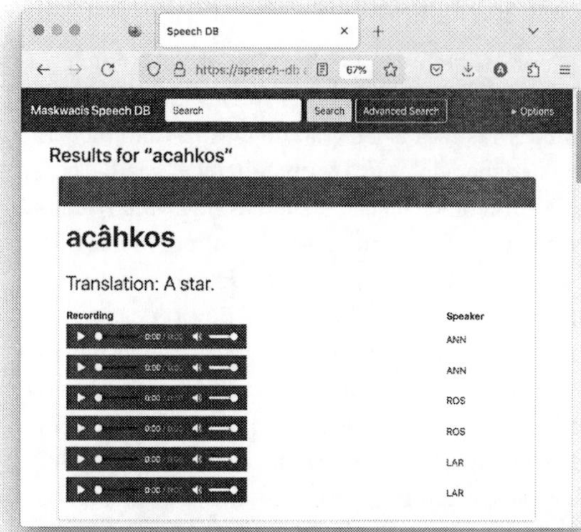

Figure 1: The entry "acâhkos" as viewed by a user who is not logged in.

4 Description of the application

4.1 User types and functionality

The Speech-DB supports six distinct user types, implemented so as to segment permissions and authorizations. The first of these user types are Unauthorized users; that is, users who are not logged in to a Speech-DB account. Such users can see all publicly available language families and can view and listen to all recordings belonging to those families. They have zero permissions to provide feedback or make any changes to the database, and are shown minimal metadata information for each entry (Figure 1).

The second user type is designated as 'Learners'. These users, who must be logged into an account, have access to all features available to unauthorized users, with the addition of being able to flag entries for review. This allows Learner users, who are assumed to be neither fluent speakers nor linguists, to provide feedback on entries without making any direct changes to the database. An internal Issue is created for each flagged entry, storing the feedback from the user. Issues can then be reviewed and addressed by more advanced users. In addition, Learners can record new audio directly into the Speech-DB, subject to review by linguists.

The third user type is that of the 'Instructor'. Currently, Instructors have the same privileges as Learners. In the future, Instructors will receive access to specific layouts and displays intended for instructing the language, such as the option to view entries grouped by lesson type or complexity.

The fourth level of access is the 'Language Expert'. Language Experts, assumed to be native or otherwise fluent speakers, have more available options than Instructors, and are shown additional metadata for each entry (Figure 2). In addition to flagging entries for review and adding new entries to the database, Language Experts can validate the recording quality of existing entries. Validation is done through a series of steps, each involving its own button or pair of buttons on the entry. Firstly, the Language Expert can indicate if the transcription and translation are both spelled correctly and if the meanings are correct through the use of "Yes", "No", and "I don't know" buttons. The last option is provided so as not to oblige users to accept or reject entries with which they are not familiar. This option also informs the site administrators which entries require further review. Next, the Language Expert can listen to each recording for the entry, marking them as "Good" or "Bad" based both on recording quality and quality of pronunciation. These changes are directly reflected in the database. While listening to the recordings, Language Experts can note if the Cree word(s) in the recording do not match the transcription (but are otherwise valid), or if a recording is assigned to the incorrect speaker, using a series of buttons on each entry. These issues are logged as Issue items and can be reviewed by either Language Expert users or linguists.

'Linguists' constitute the fifth user group, and

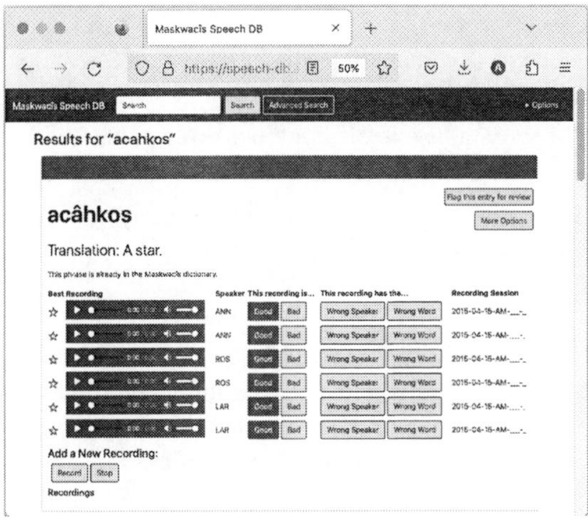

Figure 2: The entry "acâhkos" as viewed by a Language Expert level user.

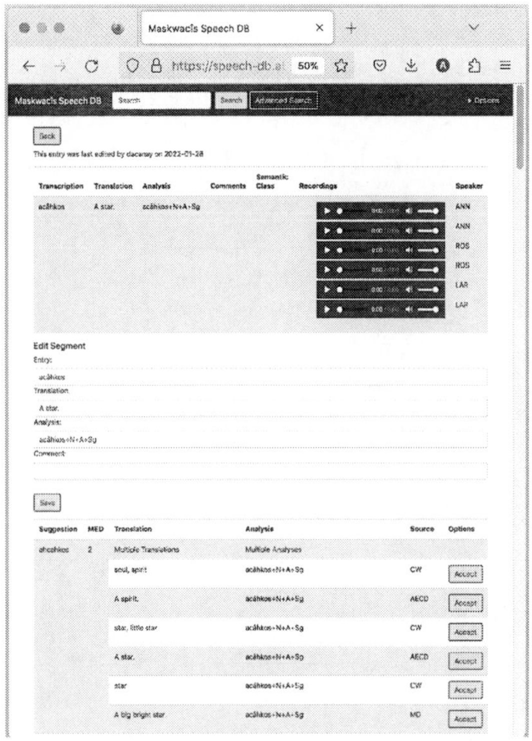

Figure 3: The top section of the "More Options" page, accessible only to Linguist level users, for the entry "acâhkos". Features the entry metadata and recordings as well as the top items in the suggestions table.

have identical permissions as Language Experts, with the additional option to view and alter interlinear glosses, translations, and transcriptions directly using a button labeled "More Options" (Figure 3). This option allows 'Linguist' users to make changes directly to the database. When available, transcription, translation, and analysis suggestions are provided through the use of a finite-state morphological model (for Plains Cree, described in Snoek et al. (2014) and Harrigan et al. (2017)) and dictionary content from the sister application *itwêwina*. Suggestions are ranked by *Modified Edit Distance* (MED), which the service calculates itself. An entry's MED is the number of changes needed for the suggestion to match the current input. The MED assigns a lesser penalty to some common inconsistencies in the spelling of Plains Cree words that we are aware of; for other spelling divergences the regular edit distance penalty is applied. For example, adding or removing an 'i' or an 'h' has a distance of 0.5, thus 0.5 is added to the total MED for every 'i' or 'h' that is added or removed from the original entry in order to match the suggested entry. Adding or removing a diacritic from a character has a cost of 0, whereas adding or removing any letter other than 'i' or 'h' has a cost of 1. All these changes are calculated and summed up to present the total MED between the current transcription and the suggested spelling. Lastly, this Linguist-specific view contains a table listing all previous changes made to an entry, when those changes were made, and by whom the changes were made (Figure 4). This table can then be used to revert an entry to a previous state in the case that it was incorrectly changed at some point in history.

The sixth and final user type is the 'Administrator', a role reserved for one or two software-educated users who update the database in the backend and make changes to the service using Django's Administrator interface. The role has no special privileges on the front-end and has total control over the backend, with the ability to change any and all aspects of any given entry.

As previously mentioned, many user-types have the ability to record new entries directly into the Speech-DB. This can be done either from the entry itself, which then adds a new provisional recording to the database containing the transcription and translation of that entry, or through the page directly intended for recording new entries. In the latter option, the transcription and translation are added in text fields before the user records as many entries as desired, saving only the ones that meet their standards of pronunciation and audio quality. If this user has recorded entries in the past, there will be a "speaker" object associated with the user

Figure 4: The bottom end of the "More Options" page, accessible only to Linguist level users, for the entry "acâhkos". Features the end of the suggestions table and the revisions table.

and this speaker object will be used. Otherwise, a new speaker object is made using the name and username provided when the account was created.

4.2 Technical specifications

The entire Speech-DB code-base is available as open source in: `https://github.com/UAlbertaALTLab/recording-validation-interface`. The service is a Django monoserver, in that it uses Python's Django as both the backend and frontend components. The backend handles all the logic of importing new recordings, storing newly-recorded entries, and handling user input. The frontend displays all the information and options to the user using the Django framework and templates. All the information is stored on a server, which serves the site to the public using uwsgi and nginx, and the data themselves are stored in a sqlite3 database. This server is housed on a server provided by Digital Research Alliance of Canada, running Ubuntu and serving the sites to nginx using Docker. Audio information is kept on the server in its original .wav quality format, but it is also converted into .mp4 format at the time it is added to the database as this format is smaller and easier to serve over the web.

The database itself contains seven tables with an additional eight relational tables to store all the information. The seven main tables are for storing Issues, as discussed above, language variants or language families for each new language pair that is supported by the Speech-DB, phrases, recordings, recording sessions, semantic classes, and speakers. Speakers are either users who have recorded an entry, or manually entered names of people who have contributed to the database. Adding a new language pair is as simple as adding a new entry to the language variant table, which takes maximally five minutes. Entries and speakers are then associated with this new language family and only presented to users when viewing the entries for that language family.

When another service, such as *itwêwina*, requests a recording from Speech-DB, it makes a GET request to the bulk recording API built into the back-end of Speech-DB. This API endpoint can accept up to 30 query terms and returns a JSON object containing the terms that were found in the database along with a separate list of terms that were not found in the database. For every entry found in the Speech-DB, a list of the corresponding recordings is returned with the name of the word. When searching for words, each instantiation of *itwêwina* contains the community code, which is found in the URL of any language family's main content (e.g., the code for Maskwacîs is "maskwacis", a URL-safe version of the name), and each of those URLs are queried for the term. In the case of Plains Cree, the Speech-DB needs to account for potential spelling variations, mainly using macrons, <ē>, instead of circumflexes, <ê>, or in some cases neither diacritic, <e>. To accommodate any such spellings, each query is done with each set of characters and then the entry associated with the recording is correctly assigned back to the initial query term by undoing the changes done to the accent marker.

This exchange between Speech-DB and another service allows for the presentation of spoken forms for individual words, or their collections as organized into "spoken paradigms", both types exemplified in Figure 5 (for the entry "nipâw"[1]).

[1] `https://itwewina.altlab.app/word/nipÃćw/?paradigm-size=full`

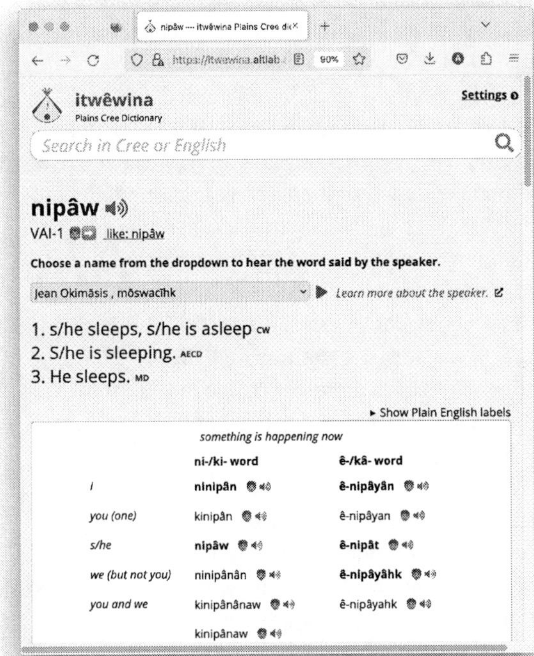

Figure 5: The presentation of spoken recordings for both the individual Cree search term "nipâw" and a collection of audio organized into a "spoken paradigm", fetched from Speech-DB to another on-line application, namely *itwêwina*. The recordings can be played by toggling the speaker icons, which, when paired with a human face icon, indicate a human recording (in contrast to synthesized audio).

4.3 New features

In addition to its current features, the Speech-DB will soon see numerous expansions in the form of new features. The first of such features is the completion of the possibility to search for entries based on their semantic classifications, which is currently only partially implemented. This feature will be expanded to include classifications made using WordNet (Miller et al., 1993; Dacanay et al., 2021) as well as more accurate RapidWords classifications. The ability to include hypernyms and hyponyms for WordNet classifications will also be added to this search functionality.

Next, the ability to start a new database with RapidWords prompts will be added. While this is currently theoretically possible, in order to accomplish it, the software developer must add all these entries by running a script on the database. This new feature would allow users to select a flag when creating a new language family that automatically populates the database with prompts from RapidWords, or indeed any other written and codified semantic domain set. Subsequently, the previously mentioned table of spelling and analysis suggestions accompanied by a MED only works on single word phrases. We would hope to expand this functionality into multi-word phrases and have suggested spellings and analyses for each component of the phrase.

Lastly, users have requested the ability to bulk change a particular speaker code for a particular session. This is necessary due to occasional errors in the initial recording sessions, in which certain speaker codes were erroneously miscoded. When such errors occur, users must change the speaker code of every incorrectly-coded recording individually. However, users will eventually have the ability to change speaker codes in bulk, shifting speaker A for speaker B for an entire session.

5 Work processes by current users

As mentioned, the basic standardization and validation processes for which Speech-DB was designed may be exemplified in the undertaking of these processes for the Maskwacîs Cree audio, which (at the time that it was initially uploaded to Speech-DB) was aligned with transcriptions and translations taken from the field elicitation sheets and notes produced by the linguists who collected the audio. These elicitation notes were organized under semantic groupings following Rapid Words, and combined semantically classified content from the Maskwacîs Cree Dictionary (which did not adhere to Standard Roman Orthography (Okimāsis and Wolvengrey, 2008), as well as "new" Cree words and sentences in response to prompt questions and words throughout the elicitation session. As the multiple linguists recording the sessions were not fluent speakers of Plains Cree, the written records represented their best approximation of the phonological form of what they heard, rather than the orthographically standard form. The resultant transcriptions therefore required comprehensive orthographic standardization. Furthermore, the English translations varied, either following conventions in the *Maskwacîs Cree Dictionary* (Maskwachees Cultural College, 2009) or the larger *Cree: Words* dictionary (Wolvengrey, 2011), or some hybrid of both; these too were to be standardized.

To facilitate this standardization, the Maskwacîs

Cree audio clips were uploaded to the Speech-DB and grouped by the elicitation session in which they were collected (which would concern words mainly from related semantic domains). These sets of recordings were then manually reviewed by a linguist with knowledge of Plains Cree morphosyntax and orthographic conventions (initially the third author, and then primarily the second author). For each entry, the linguist would, using the provided recordings, verify that the word or sentence spoken in the audio was the word or sentence provided in the gloss. The linguist would subsequently standardize the spelling of the Cree words in the 'Transcription' field to SRO conventions, render the definition in the 'Translation' field to a format closely resembling that used in the largest currently existing Plains Cree dictionary (Wolvengrey, 2011), and provide an interlinear gloss detailing the inflectional characteristics of the word(s) present in the 'Analysis' field, making use of the computationally generated suggestions when suitable. A fourth field, the 'Comments' field, was used in instances in which the entry in question was notable or unusual in some respect; typically, in the process of standardization, this was reserved for alternative spellings, derivational breakdowns of semantically non-compositional terms, and morphosyntactic irregularities. However, this 'Comments' field (which was added to the site by the request of linguists working with Speech-DB) was also used as a miscellaneous repository for additional information on entries.

After being manually standardized and interlinearized by a linguist, the quality of the recordings and translations for these entries were also validated by Rose Makinaw, an L1 Cree-speaking elder from Maskwacîs, in collaboration with linguists (second and third author) and the software developer (first author). Across 162 validation sessions, totalling 262 hours, these audio validations have covered 50% of the total contents of the Speech-DB, as well as having provided 500 novel words to the database with multiple recordings of each.

6 Feedback from current users

In total, using Speech-DB as an editing interface, the second author has been able to standardize roughly 63% of the 20,299 entries of Maskwacîs Cree over the course of 21 months of sporadic work. He has noted no significant structural deficits with Speech-DB as a platform (with the exception of occasional server errors), and deemed the general layout as "intuitive" and as "not requiring a great deal of training to use".

Furthermore, the aforementioned native Cree speaker (who has no formal training in linguistics and a self-professed lack of tact in the use of computers and digital interfaces) reported no complaints regarding the practical usage of the site, and commented that she was "comfortable with it" after having been exposed to it for a time. When asked about how she would explain the interface to a new user, she commented that it would be sufficient to have them "sit beside me" during a validation session, and described her own experience of learning to use the site as "not that bad". When asked what skills a potential validation annotator using Speech-DB would need to begin their work, she mentioned only literacy in the Cree Standard Roman Orthography and for the annotator to be "fluent enough to know when ... the speakers [on the database] are saying it wrong"; no mention of specialized computational or linguistic knowledge was mentioned.

The software developer (first author) has participated in a large proportion of the validation sessions, from their beginning in March 2021 until the time of writing, in order to directly observe any erroneous or otherwise undesirable functionality, and consequently to resolve such issues as swiftly as possible. Several of the linguists involved in the initial recordings have also participated, and have consistently judged that the validation and associated standardization activities currently undertaken in Speech-DB are being accomplished as efficiently as can be reasonably expected while still giving each and every recording, transcription, and translation a sufficient amount of attention for proper quality assurance. Indeed, while the very first 10 validation sessions involved a learning process and covered on average 13 entries per hour, at the end of that period the rate had already increased to 25 entries/hour, having now doubled to 60 entries/hour. As for the standardization work, that has always progressed faster than validation, and has now reached a rate of 110 entries/hour.

7 Comparison with other relevant similar applications

Although other applications similar to the Speech-DB exist, none of the ones we are aware of are able to fill all of the aforementioned usage roles.

Feature / Application	**Speech-DB**	**DGD2** (Schmidt, 2014)	**Talk-Bank** (MacWhinney, 2019)	**Library of Congress (1986/2023)**
Add new recordings	+	–	+	–
Validate existing recordings	+	–	–	–
Authenticate users	+	+	–	–
Add linguistic analyses to entries	+	–	?	–
Publicly view entries	+	+	+	+
Easily access recordings from other services	+	–	?	?
Search for recordings	+	+	–	+
Intended for language preservation, documentation, and exploration	+	–	–	–

Table 1: A comparison of the Speech-DB with other similar services.

Table 1 shows a comparison of the Speech-DB with three other similar services.

While these other services all existed at the time the Speech-DB was created, they differ in several respects. Foremost among these are the intentions of the service. The Speech-DB was custom designed based on a set of criteria aimed at documenting and preserving the language, which none of the other services have as their aim, nor do they offer some of the key elements the Speech-DB does provide, such as the ability to validate entries and access them from other services on the Internet.

8 Conclusion

The Speech-DB is an online platform for spoken language data available to the public in varying degrees of access, depending on the user's familiarity with the language. It serves as a service for documentation, exploration, and validation, with its functionalities having expanded over time to accommodate user needs. The primary users of Speech-DB regard it as easy to use and generally have no complaints about how it operates. The Speech-DB differs from other similar platforms primarily in its ability to grow and adapt with the language, easily add new language families, and easily add new recordings.

Limitations

Although Speech-DB can be used as a standalone exploratory tool for language learners, using it for extensive, rich documentation (of the kind outlined for Plains Cree) does require some degree of linguistic understanding, in that such an extent of analysis of the data necessitates the establishment or implementation of some form of coding convention for the linguistic features apparent in the entries, and/or the existence of a computational model/parser that can suggest such analyses. As such, although language community members can act largely independently in creating and populating a Speech-DB for their own language, the contribution of linguists may be needed for more advanced linguistic analysis. Furthermore, Speech-DB has been primarily used for analyzing and validating pre-existing recordings, which had been collected and processed separately, rather than solely recording the audio using Speech-DB; instead, Speech-DB was used afterwards for recording individual additional audio, when considered necessary. For more extensive recording projects using solely Speech-DB, the application would yet benefit from stream-lining the recording process to better support the recording of larger batches of vocabulary in a convenient and efficient fashion. Additionally, while Speech-DB provides the framework to allow users to search by categories such as semantic domain, such categories do require the provision of additional information when entries are initially added or recorded.

Ethics Statement

The collection of audio which is stored and made available in Speech-DB is covered by an ethics review and approval at the University of Alberta (Study ID: Pro00023436). The platform described in this manuscript has been developed in order to support the explicit objectives of the language communities in question to record how their language is spoken in their communities and make that available for their next generations.

Acknowledgements

Creating a useful application that supports the revitalization of Plains Cree (*nêhiyawêwin*) is a task that relies on the knowledge, time, and goodwill of many people. We thank the Social Sciences and Humanities Research Council (SSHRC) for their Partnership Development Grant (#890-2013-0047), Connections Grant (#611-2016-0207), and Partnership Grant (#895-2019-1012) for supporting this project over the last decade, and are equally grateful for the Research Cluster Grant from the Kule Institute for Advanced Study (KIAS), University of Alberta. Earlier stages of the software development were supported by Eddie Antonio Santos and Andrew Neitsch. We would especially like to thank the staff at Miyo Wahkohtowin Education, now part of Maskwacîs Education Schools Community (MESC), for their wonderful enthusiasm, and for welcoming us into their community. In particular we want to note Brian Wildcat, Patricia Johnson, and Rose Makinaw, who were instrumental in ensuring the recording project would be carried out. The actual recordings were faciliated by Atticus Harrigan, Katherine Schmirler, Dustin Bowers, Megan Bontogon, and a number of other students at the University of Alberta. We would also like to acknowledge the crucial advice, attention, and effort of Jean Okimâsis and Arok Wolvengrey from First Nations University of Canada. Last but by no means least, we are indebted to all the Elders and native speakers of Plains Cree in Maskwacîs, enumerated in Littlechild et al., 2018. and in `https://speech-db.altlab.app/maskwacis/speakers/`, for the countless hours of their time that they contributed to creating the content of the Spoken Dictionary of Maskwacîs Cree, which we are today fortunate to be able to make available through the Speech-DB.

References

Antti Arppe, Atticus Harrigan, Katherine Schmirler, and Arok Wolvengrey. 2018. A morphologically intelligent online dictionary for Plains Cree. In *Stabilizing Indigenous Languages Symposium (SILS2018)*, University of Lethbridge, Alberta, June 7-9, 2018.

Antti Arppe, Jolene Poulin, Atticus Harrigan, Katherine Schmirler, Daniel Dacanay, and Rose Makinaw. 2022a. *êkosi ê-nêhiyawi-pîkiskwêcik maskwacîsihk* – Towards a spoken dictionary of Maskwacis Cree. In *Fifty-Fourth Algonquian Conference (PAC54)*, Boulder, Colorado, October 22, 2022.

Antti Arppe, Jolene Poulin, Atticus Harrigan, Katherine Schmirler, Daniel Dacanay, and Rose Makinaw. 2022b. *êkosi ê-nêhiyawi-pîkiskwêcik maskwacîsihk* – Towards a spoken dictionary of Maskwacis Cree. In *Partnerships in Practice, Special Session at the 5th Workshop on the Use of Computational Methods in the Study of Endangered Languages (ComputEL-5)*, Dublin, Ireland, May 27, 2022.

Antti Arppe, Jolene Poulin, Eddie Antonio Santos, Andrew Neitsch, Atticus Harrigan, Katherine Schmirler, Daniel Hieber, Ansh Dubey, and Arok Wolvengrey. 2022c. *itwêwina* – Towards a morphologically intelligent and user-friendly on-line dictionary of Plains Cree – next next round. In *Fifty-Fourth Algonquian Conference (PAC54)*, Boulder, Colorado, October 22, 2022.

Brenda H. Boerger and Verna Stutzman. 2018. Single-event rapid word collection workshops: Efficient, Effective, Empowering. *Language Documentation and Conservation*, 12:147–193.

Daniel Dacanay, Atticus G. Harrigan, and Antti Arppe. 2021. Computational analysis versus human intuition: A critical comparison of vector semantics with manual semantic classification in the context of Plains Cree. In *Proceedings of the 4th Workshop on Computational Methods for Endangered Languages*, pages 33–43.

Atticus Harrigan, Antti Arppe, and Timothy Mills. 2019. Preliminary Plains Cree speech synthesizer. In *Proceedings of the 3rd Workshop on the Use of Computational Methods in the Study of Endangered Languages (ComputEL-3)*, pages 64–73, Stroudsburgh, Pennsylvania. Association of Computational Linguistics.

Atticus Harrigan, Katherine Schmirler, Antti Arppe, Lene Antonsen, Sjur N. Moshagen, Trond Trosterud, and Arok Wolvengrey. 2017. Learning from the computational modeling of Plains Cree verbs. *Morphology*, 27:565–598.

Library of Congress. 1986/2023. *American English Dialect Recordings: The Center for Applied Linguistics Collection (AFC 1986/022).*

Mary Jean Littlechild, Louise Wildcat, Jerry Roasting, Harley Simon, Annette Lee, Arlene Makinaw, Rosie Rowan, Rose Makinaw, Kisikaw, Betty Simon, Brian Lightning, Brian Lee, Linda Oldpan, Miriam Buffalo, Debora Young, Ivy Raine, Paula Mackinaw, Norma Linda Saddleback, Renee Makinaw, Atticus Harrigan, Katherine Schmirler, Dustin Bowers, Megan Bontogon, Sarah Giesbrecht, Patricia Johnson, Timothy Mills, Jordan Lachler, and Antti Arppe. 2018. Towards a spoken dictionary of Maskwacîs Cree. In *25th Stabilizing Indigenous Languages Symposium (SILS2018)*, University of Lethbridge, Alberta, June 7-9, 2018.

Brian MacWhinney. 2019. Understanding spoken language through TalkBank. *Behaviour Research Methods*, 51:1919–1927.

Maskwachees Cultural College. 2009. *Maskwacîs Dictionary of Cree Words / Nêhiyaw Pîkiskwêwinisa*. Maskwacîs, Alberta.

George A. Miller, Richard Beckwith, Christiane Fellbaum, Derek Gross, and Katherine J. Miller. 1993. Introduction to WordNet: an on-line lexical database. *International Journal of Lexicography*, 3:235–244.

Jean Okimāsis and Arok Wolvengrey. 2008. *How to Spell it in Cree: the Standard Roman Orthography*. Miywâsin Ink, Regina, Saskatchewan.

Tanzi Reule. 2018. *Elicitation and Speech Acts in the Maskwacîs Spoken Cree Dictionary Project (Honors thesis)*. Department of Linguistics, University of Alberta.

Thomas Schmidt. 2014. The database for spoken German – DGD2. In *Proceedings of the Ninth International Conference on Language Resources and Evaluation (LREC'14)*, pages 1451–1457, Reykjavik, Iceland. European Language Resources Association (ELRA).

Conor Snoek, Dorothy Thunder, Kaidi Lõo, Antti Arppe, Jordan Lachler, Juhani Järvikivi, Timothy Mills, Sjur N. Moshagen, and Trond Trosterud. 2014. Modeling the noun morphology of Plains Cree. In *Proceedings of the 2014 Workshop on the Use of Computational Methods in the Study of Endangered Languages (ComputEL)*, pages 34–42, Baltimore, Maryland, USA. Association of Computational Linguistics.

Arok Wolvengrey. 2011. *Cree : Words / nêhiyawêwin : itwêwina*. University of Regina Press, Regina, Saskatchewan.

ASR pipeline for low-resourced languages: A case study on Pomak

Chara Tsoukala Kosmas Kritsis Ioannis Douros Athanasios Katsamanis
Nikolaos Kokkas Vasileios Arampatzakis Vasileios Sevetlidis
Stella Markantonatou George Pavlidis
Institute for Language and Speech Processing, Athena R.C.
{chara.tsoukala, kosmas.kritsis, ioannis.douros, nkatsam, nikolaos.kokkas, vasilis.arampatzakis, vasiseve, marks, gpavlid}@athenarc.gr

Abstract

Automatic Speech Recognition (ASR) models can aid field linguists by facilitating the creation of text corpora from oral material. Training ASR systems for low-resource languages can be a challenging task not only due to lack of resources but also due to the work required for the preparation of a training dataset. We present a pipeline for data processing and ASR model training for low-resourced languages, based on the language family. As a case study, we collected recordings of Pomak, an endangered South East Slavic language variety spoken in Greece. Using the proposed pipeline, we trained the first Pomak ASR model.

1 Introduction

Speech technologies have gained popularity in the past decade and several people use voice commands to communicate with their devices or to dictate messages. Furthermore, such technologies can be of use in field and corpus linguistics. Manually transcribing one minute of recorded speech takes on average 40 minutes; Automatic Speech Recognition (ASR) models can facilitate the transcription of spoken corpora by providing the first iteration of the transcription (Foley et al., 2018). If high-quality recordings are available, Text-to-Speech (TTS) models can augment speech corpora by generating audio files from text.

However, training robust models requires several hundred hours of recorded speech, while most languages do not have enough such resources. Therefore, in low-resource settings, one typically bootstraps the process using a model that has been pre-trained in a related language with sufficient resources (e.g., wav2vec2 (Baevski et al., 2020), XLS-R (Conneau et al., 2021), and Whisper (Radford et al., 2022)). The pre-trained model is then fine-tuned on the target language data to obtain the final model (e.g., (Khare et al., 2021; Baevski et al., 2020; Hjortnaes et al., 2020)). To aid linguists, Foley et al. (2018) proposed a pipeline ("Elpis") to help train a Kaldi-based (Povey et al., 2011) ASR model with minimal scripting. The pipeline assumes that the transcription has been done via ELAN [1] which includes timestamps.

However, in case the available transcriptions lack time annotations, creating a dataset for a low-resource language can be a demanding task; one of the reasons is that, typically, ASR systems require short audio segments for the training process. Therefore, to create a dataset, any available recordings must be segmented into smaller parts while retaining the corresponding transcription. Splitting an audio file on its own is a relatively straightforward task in specific conditions. One can use, for instance, a Voice Activity Detection (VAD) algorithm (e.g., using PyAnnote (Bredin and Laurent, 2021) or Praat[2] (Boersma and Van Heuven, 2001)) that segments based on whether speech is present in the signal. However, in the case of missing audio-transcription time alignments, VAD alone cannot split the transcription.

We propose a pipeline (Section 2) for low-resourced languages that i) normalizes the available audio and transcription files, ii) extracts speech-text word-level alignments, iii) segments the audio files into smaller parts to create a dataset, and iv) fine-tunes an ASR model based on the language family. As a use case, we have focused on Pomak, an endangered South East Slavic language variety spoken in Greece (Karahóğa et al., 2022).

Specifically, we have recorded over 14 hours of Pomak read speech (Section 3.1) and used the proposed pipeline to train the first Pomak ASR model (Section 3.2). Even though 14 hours of speech is considered a low-resourced setting in the field of Automatic Speech Recognition, for many endangered languages the available recordings are even fewer. For this reason, we further trained an

[1] https://archive.mpi.nl/tla/elan
[2] https://www.fon.hum.uva.nl/praat/

Proceedings of the Second Workshop on NLP Applications to Field Linguistics, pages 40–45
May 6, 2023

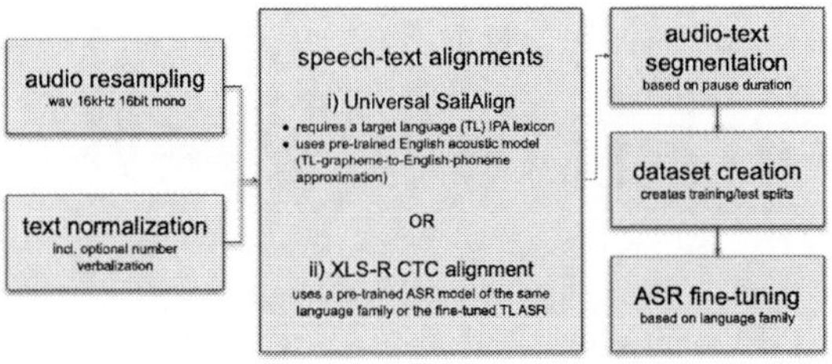

Figure 1: Proposed ASR pipeline

ASR model using only 1 hour of speech to show the applicability of the proposed approach even in the case of a simulated endangered language scenario.

2 ASR pipeline

Typically, popular ASR models use sample rates of 8kHz (8000 samples/sec) or 16kHz. The first step of the pipeline (Figure 1) is to convert all recordings to the latter sample rate (16kHz 16-bit mono channel wav files) because it provides more accurate high-frequency information and it matches the sample rate of the pre-trained models we use (see Section 2.3). Additionally, we normalize the text and convert dates and numbers to their literal equivalent.

To be able to verbalize Pomak dates and numbers, we have extended the num2words package[3]. This part is language-specific and will need to be customized for a new under-resourced language. If that is not possible, the conversion step needs to be done manually and the user will need to convert the numbers into their lexical equivalents.

The most challenging part of the data preprocessing task is the segmentation of audio files while retaining the correct transcription of words. To do so, we first need to obtain speech-text alignments in order to get the exact onset and offset times of each word.

2.1 Speech-text alignments

Speech-text alignments, also known as forced alignments, require an acoustic model (AM) of the language to successfully match audio with a transcript. However, training the AM requires lots of data, which a low-resourced language does not have. To bypass this issue, we have extended SailAlign (Katsamanis et al., 2011) to be able to align new languages using an English pre-trained model.

[3]https://github.com/savoirfairelinux/num2words

Pomak	IPA	English phone
hálove	h a l o v e	hh aa l ow v eh
hadaíčko	h a d a i tʃ k o	hh aa d aa iy ch k ow
haklýje	h a k l i j e	hh aa k l iy y eh

Table 1: Examples of Pomak words, their phonetic representation, and their transformation to an English phone representation that allows SailAlign to use the pre-trained English acoustic model

2.1.1 Universal SailAlign

SailAlign is a toolkit for robust speech-text alignment of long audio files, that implements an adaptive, iterative speech recognition and text alignment scheme. It currently supports English, Spanish, and Greek.

To obtain the alignments in a new language (Pomak in this case), we provided the toolkit with a Pomak IPA dictionary and a Pomak grapheme to English phoneme approximation (see Table 1). This allowed us to utilize the pre-trained English acoustic model, without training a Pomak ASR.

Since Pomak is a Slavic language there is no perfect match between Pomak and English phonemes. However, even this approximation results in good alignments that can be used to segment the original recordings (see Section 2.1.3). The big advantage of this method is that no AM training is needed. The only input needed is the audio-transcription pairs and an IPA (pronunciation) lexicon.

Typically, the IPA lexicon is difficult to obtain because it requires that a phonetician provides the phonetic representation of several words. In case there is no IPA dictionary available in the target language, we have created a helper script that generates an approximation based on a language that has a similar phonology. More specifically, the script is based on Phonemizer (Bernard and Titeux, 2021) that employs eSpeak NG[4] TTS which supports over 100 languages. To test this method, we generated an IPA dictionary in Pomak based on the phonology of another Slavic language.

SailAlign does not handle out-of-vocabulary (OOV) words; the IPA dictionary should contain all words in the transcription files. To facilitate this process, if the user has an incomplete existing IPA dictionary (i.e., if the IPA dictionary lacks some of the words in the transcription files), the Universal SailAlign script can use Phonetisaurus (Novak et al., 2016) to generate the missing

[4]https://github.com/espeak-ng/espeak-ng

items. Phonetisaurus is an open-source grapheme-to-phoneme tool based on Weighted Finite States Transducers (WFSTs). Universal SailAlign is available at `https://gitlab.com/ilsp-spmd-all/filotis/universal_sail_align`.

2.1.2 Wav2vec2 XLS-R alignments

An alternative method of obtaining alignments is using the CTC-segmentation algorithm proposed by Kürzinger et al. (2020). This method uses a Connectionist Temporal Classification (CTC)-based end-to-end network; in this case, we are using a wav2vec2 (Baevski et al., 2020) ASR model. The model can be a pre-trained model of the same language family (e.g., Slavic), but, ideally, it should be the fine-tuned model of the target language (the process is described in Section 2.3). The advantage of this alignment method is that it is readily available once an initial ASR model is obtained. However, the process heavily depends on the model used; especially when using a generic pre-trained model, alignment success is not guaranteed, making it a less reliable alignment method than Universal SailAlign for low-resourced languages.

2.1.3 Manual evaluation of alignments

To evaluate the performance of the alignments, we manually corrected a few Pomak alignment files and compared the performance of Universal SailAlign and wav2vec2 XLS-R alignments. Specifically, we sampled four audio files of a total of 20 minutes. Using the corresponding Universal SailAlign alignment files as a baseline, we manually corrected the generated alignments using Audacity[5]. As displayed in Figure 2, the percentage of correctly aligned words is at peak for tolerance durations larger than 0.2 seconds, i.e., when the automatically aligned boundaries are considered correct even if they differ up to 200 milliseconds from the manually corrected ones. For smaller time differences (i.e., a tolerance alignment of 0.1 seconds and below), Universal SailAlign clearly outperforms the XLS-R alignments. [6]

2.2 Audio segments

As mentioned above, ASR systems require short audio segments as training input. Typically, audio segments of up to 30 seconds are used to train or fine-tune a model.

[5]Audacity is an open-source audio and label editor. www.audacityteam.org/

[6]The results are available at `https://osf.io/dkbnu`

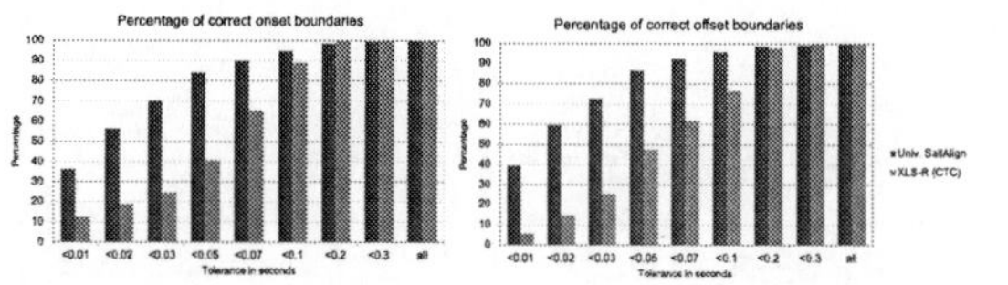

Figure 2: Percentage of correct alignments for Universal SailAlign (Section 2.1.1) and XLS-R (Section 2.1.2)

Speaker	Gender	Total recording duration
NK9dIF	F	4h 44m 45s
xoVY9q	M	4h 36m 12s
9G75fk	F	1h 44m 03s
n5WzHj	M	3h 44m 04s

Table 2: Total recording duration per speaker for the original (i.e., pre-segmented) recordings

To be able to split the audio files while retaining their transcription, we use the alignment files from Section 2.1. We split the files based on i) a silence duration threshold between two words ("pause duration"), which we set to 0.3 and ii) a minimum number of words per segment, which we set to two [7]. Campione and Véronis (2002) studied silent pause durations based on the analysis of 5 ½ hours of speech in five Indo-European languages, and categorized silences in brief (< 0.2s), medium (0.2 - 1s) and long (> 1s) pauses. Therefore, we suggest using a pause duration threshold between 0.2 and 1 second to segment the audio.

The final step of the data processing pipeline splits the audio segments-transcription pairs into a training, validation, and test dataset (80-10-10 respectively).

2.3 ASR fine-tuning

As mentioned in the introduction, in low-resource settings one typically fine-tunes a model that has been pre-trained on several hundred hours of a related language. In our pipeline, we are using a language-family-specific version of the wav2vec2 XLS-R model (Babu et al., 2022) that has been exposed to 56k hours in 53 languages[8]. The script that allows one to create a dataset and fine-tune a HuggingFace XLS-R model based on the language family is available at `https://gitlab.com/ilsp-spmd-all/filotis/speech_to_text`.

[7]The segmentor is available at `https://gitlab.com/ilsp-spmd-all/filotis/silent-pause-segmentation`

[8]huggingface.co/facebook/wav2vec2-large-xlsr-53

Model	WER	CER
Slavic model		
Fine-tuned	9.06	3.12
Baseline	87.31	31.47
Multilingual model		
Fine-tuned	12.43	3.90
Baseline	97.27	49.77

Table 3: ASR error rates for pre-trained ('Baseline') and fine-tuned Slavic and multilingual models (11h Pomak segments)

3 The case of Pomak

3.1 Recordings

Pomak has a rather weak online presence, which typically involves folk singing, so we could not simply crawl the web to create a dataset; only a few texts, and even fewer recordings, are available online. For instance, Salakidis et al. (2016) collected a few songs, recipes, and lullabies from the area of Thrace, including the Pomak community[9].

To build a Pomak corpus, we collected texts from different authors and sources (e.g., blogs and books) and included various genres (e.g. news items, folk tales, essays, biographical texts, short stories). We asked 4 native Pomak speakers to read the texts at the ILSP audio-visual studio in Xanthi, Greece. Pomak does not have an official script; the few existing texts are written in various alphabets: Cyrillic, Greek, IPA, and variations of the Latin alphabet (Karahóǧa et al., 2022). For uniformity, all texts were converted to the alphabet presented in Karahóǧa et al.

The duration of each recording ranges from 20 to 846 seconds, resulting in a total of over 14 hours. The total recording duration per speaker is displayed in Table 2. We also recorded a short free dialogue (4m 33s) between the two male speakers which we transcribed and added to the dataset.

3.2 ASR experiments: Low-resourced and endangered scenario

Using the proposed pipeline, we created a Pomak dataset to train our ASR model. Note that smaller segments also mean fewer pauses in the dataset. This results in a reduction of the total audio duration: The final duration of the audio files is 11 hours and 8 minutes in total.

[9]Their recordings are available at `http://ct-audiolink.eee.uniwa.gr/`

Slavic model	WER	CER
Fine-tuned (11 hours)	8.57	2.31
Fine-tuned (1 hour)	18.15	4.59
Baseline	87.14	30.13

Table 4: ASR model results on the 1-hour dataset split for the full fine-tuned model (11 hours), mini fine-tuned model (1 hour) and pre-trained Slavic model (baseline).

To obtain a Pomak ASR model, we fine-tuned existing XLS-R models for 35 epochs[10] using the Pomak segments. Specifically, we fine-tuned i) an XLS-R model that had been exposed to Slavic languages (Ljubešić et al., 2022) ("Slavic model"[11]) and ii) an XLS-R model that had been exposed to 56 languages of the Common Voice dataset ("multilingual model"[12]). The results can be seen in Table 3. The fine-tuned Slavic model (i.e., the Slavic model that was further fine-tuned on the Pomak training set) has the lowest Word Error Rate (WER) and Character Error Rate (CER) on the test set. The multilingual model has a higher error rate, although it can also be useful if there is no language-family-specific pre-trained model available for the target language. The test set error rates of the pre-trained models are also given as a baseline and the best Pomak model (i.e., "Slavic fine-tuned") is available at `https://huggingface.co/ilsp/wav2vec2-xls-r-slavic-pomak`.

As for endangered languages, available recordings may consist of a few minutes or hours in total. Thus, we repeated the training using only one hour of speech. Specifically, we split the test set from Table 3 into three parts: training, validation, and test. In this new sub-dataset, the total recordings per speaker ranged from 13 to 20 minutes. We repeated the fine-tuning process of the baseline Slavic model for 35 epochs. While the error rates are higher than those reported in the full 11-hour model, the results are promising even with one hour of recorded speech (Table 4). Note that the 1h-dataset split is different than the 11h-dataset split reported in Table 3, therefore the baseline and fine-tuned error rates are also slightly different.

[10]We initially fine-tuned for 100 epochs; the best checkpoints, based on the validation WER, were between the 30th and 40th epoch.

[11]The pre-trained (Baseline) Slavic model we selected is available at: `https://huggingface.co/classla/wav2vec2-xls-r-parlaspeech-hr`

[12]Pre-trained multilingual model: `https://huggingface.co/voidful/wav2vec2-xlsr-multilingual-56`

4 Conclusion

We presented a pipeline that facilitates data processing and enables ASR model training for low-resourced languages. Using this pipeline, we created the first transcription model in Pomak. We used the same dataset to train a TTS model, which we plan on using to augment the Pomak corpus.

Limitations

While we are confident that this pipeline can work for most low-resource languages, we have only tested it with Pomak, which belongs to the Slavic language family. Hugging face does not currently have pre-trained models for all language families (e.g., for indic). Therefore, for some low-resourced languages, a more generic (e.g., multilingual) pre-trained model will be selected, which will likely result in a higher error rate as shown in Table 3. Furthermore, as mentioned in Section 2.1, the wav2vec2 XLS-R-based alignments are heavily dependent on the ASR model used, while the Universal SailAlign-based alignments require an IPA dictionary of the target language. We have proposed a solution using a phonetic dictionary approximation, but this approach may also lack accuracy and it requires some manual verification. Last, the audio samples we used were of high quality as they were recorded in a studio. Noisy recordings are likely to result in less accurate i) alignments, ii) segmentations, and therefore iii) higher error rates.

Ethics Statement

All four participants have signed an informed consent form with Athena R.C. for their contribution to the narration of the voice samples.

Acknowledgements

We acknowledge support of this work by the project "PHILOTIS: State-of-the-art technologies for the recording, analysis and documentation of living languages" (MIS 5047429), which is implemented under the "Action for the Support of Regional Excellence", funded by the Operational Programme "Competitiveness, Entrepreneurship and Innovation" (NSRF 2014-2020) and co-financed by Greece and the European Union (European Regional Development Fund).

References

Arun Babu, Changhan Wang, Andros Tjandra, Kushal Lakhotia, Qiantong Xu, Naman Goyal, Kritika Singh, Patrick von Platen, Yatharth Saraf, Juan Pino, Alexei Baevski, Alexis Conneau, and Michael Auli. 2022. XLS-R: Self-supervised Cross-lingual Speech Representation Learning at Scale. In *Proc. Interspeech 2022*, pages 2278–2282.

Alexei Baevski, Yuhao Zhou, Abdelrahman Mohamed, and Michael Auli. 2020. wav2vec 2.0: A framework for self-supervised learning of speech representations. *Advances in Neural Information Processing Systems*, 33:12449–12460.

Mathieu Bernard and Hadrien Titeux. 2021. Phonemizer: Text to phones transcription for multiple languages in python. *Journal of Open Source Software*, 6(68):3958.

Paul Boersma and Vincent Van Heuven. 2001. Speak and unspeak with praat. *Glot International*, 5(9/10):341–347.

Hervé Bredin and Antoine Laurent. 2021. End-to-end speaker segmentation for overlap-aware resegmentation. In *Interspeech*.

Estelle Campione and Jean Véronis. 2002. A large-scale multilingual study of silent pause duration. In *Speech prosody 2002, international conference*.

Alexis Conneau, Alexei Baevski, Ronan Collobert, Abdelrahman Mohamed, and Michael Auli. 2021. Unsupervised Cross-Lingual Representation Learning for Speech Recognition. In *Proc. Interspeech 2021*, pages 2426–2430.

Ben Foley, Joshua T Arnold, Rolando Coto-Solano, Gautier Durantin, T Mark Ellison, Daan van Esch, Scott Heath, Frantisek Kratochvil, Zara Maxwell-Smith, David Nash, Ola Olsson, Mark Richards, Nay San, Hywel Stoakes, Nick Thieberger, and Janet Wiles. 2018. Building speech recognition systems for language documentation: The coedl endangered language pipeline and inference system (elpis). In *In S. S. Agrawal (Ed.), The 6th Intl. Workshop on Spoken Language Technologies for Under-Resourced Languages (SLTU)*, pages 205–209.

Nils Hjortnaes, Niko Partanen, Michael Rießler, and Francis M Tyers. 2020. Towards a speech recognizer for komi, an endangered and low-resource uralic language. In *Proceedings of the Sixth International Workshop on Computational Linguistics of Uralic Languages*, pages 31–37.

Ritván Jusúf Karahóğa, Panagiotis G Krimpas, Vivian Stamou, Vasileios Arampatzakis, Dimitrios Karamatskos, Vasileios Sevetlidis, Nikolaos Constantinides, Nikolaos Kokkas, George Pavlidis, and Stella Markantonatou. 2022. Morphologically annotated corpora of pomak. In *Proceedings of the Fifth Workshop on the Use of Computational Methods in the Study of Endangered Languages*, pages 179–186.

Athanasios Katsamanis, Matthew Black, Panayiotis G Georgiou, Louis Goldstein, and Shrikanth Narayanan. 2011. Sailalign: Robust long speech-text alignment. In *Proc. of workshop on new tools and methods for very-large scale phonetics research*.

Shreya Khare, Ashish R Mittal, Anuj Diwan, Sunita Sarawagi, Preethi Jyothi, and Samarth Bharadwaj. 2021. Low resource asr: The surprising effectiveness of high resource transliteration. In *Interspeech*, pages 1529–1533.

Ludwig Kürzinger, Dominik Winkelbauer, Lujun Li, Tobias Watzel, and Gerhard Rigoll. 2020. Ctc-segmentation of large corpora for german end-to-end speech recognition. In *Speech and Computer: 22nd International Conference, SPECOM 2020, St. Petersburg, Russia, October 7–9, 2020, Proceedings 22*, pages 267–278. Springer.

Nikola Ljubešić, Danijel Koržinek, Peter Rupnik, and Ivo-Pavao Jazbec. 2022. Parlaspeech-hr - a freely available asr dataset for croatian bootstrapped from the parlamint corpus. In *Proceedings of the Workshop ParlaCLARIN III within the 13th Language Resources and Evaluation Conference*, pages 111–116.

Josef Robert Novak, Nobuaki Minematsu, and Keikichi Hirose. 2016. Phonetisaurus: Exploring grapheme-to-phoneme conversion with joint n-gram models in the wfst framework. *Natural Language Engineering*, 22(6):907–938.

Daniel Povey, Arnab Ghoshal, Gilles Boulianne, Lukas Burget, Ondrej Glembek, Nagendra Goel, Mirko Hannemann, Petr Motlicek, Yanmin Qian, Petr Schwarz, et al. 2011. The kaldi speech recognition toolkit. In *IEEE 2011 workshop on automatic speech recognition and understanding*, CONF. IEEE Signal Processing Society.

Alec Radford, Jong Wook Kim, Tao Xu, Greg Brockman, Christine McLeavey, and Ilya Sutskever. 2022. Robust speech recognition via large-scale weak supervision. *arXiv preprint arXiv:2212.04356*.

Georgios Salakidis, Evagelia Thomadaki, Christina Markou, Theodoros Kontogiorgis, Gavriil Kamaris, and John Mourjopoulos. 2016. A database of narrations and songs recordings with cultural interest from the area of thrace. In *8th conference 'Ακουστικη'*, pages 149–157.

Improving Low-resource RRG Parsing with Structured Gloss Embeddings

Roland Eibers and **Kilian Evang** and **Laura Kallmeyer**
Heinrich Heine University Düsseldorf
Universitätsstr. 1, 40225 Düsseldorf, Germany
firstname.lastname@hhu.de

Abstract

Treebanking for local languages is hampered by the lack of existing parsers to generate pre-annotations. However, it has been shown that reasonably accurate parsers can be bootstrapped with little initial training data when use is made of the information in interlinear glosses and translations that language documentation data for such treebanks typically comes with. In this paper, we improve upon such a bootstrapping model by representing glosses using a combination of morphological feature vectors and pre-trained lemma embeddings. We also contribute a mapping from glosses to Universal Dependencies morphological features.

1 Introduction

Treebanking (i.e., annotating large corpora of sentences with syntactic structures) is an important tool for research into the syntax of natural language. Treebanking has long avoided starting from scratch, but used machine-generated pre-annotations that annotators correct (Marcus et al., 1993). For standardized languages, models generating the pre-annotations can nowadays rely on large language models and pre-trained parsers (e.g., Tyers et al., 2018; Jónsdóttir and Ingason, 2020; Bladier et al., 2022). For local languages, the situation looks quite different: usually, no large language models or other models are available. However, if the language is documented, the data usually comes with interlinear glosses and translations to a standardized language such as English (Lehmann, 1982). Evang et al. (2022) show that these annotations can be used to obtain more accurate pre-annotations for local-language treebanks by projecting contextualized word representations from a parser for English onto the target-language sentences, using character-based gloss embeddings, and self-training. In this paper, we show that the accuracy can be further improved by using a more structured representation for glosses. Our contributions are 1) a mapping from interlinear glosses to Universal Dependencies features that can be reused for other language documentation data, 2) based on that, a method for embedding glossed sentences using morphological feature vectors and lemma embeddings, and 3) an evaluation of this embedding method in the context of cross-lingual RRG parsing for treebank pre-annotation.

2 Related work

Low-resource RRG parsing Evang et al. (2022) consider the task of creating pre-annotations for treebanks for the Oceanic local languages Daakaka and Dalkalaen. The annotation scheme is based on that of RRGparbank (Bladier et al., 2022), following Role and Reference Grammar (RRG; Van Valin and Foley, 1980; Van Valin, 2005), a framework designed with diverse languages in mind. The text data for the treebanks comes with interlinear glosses and English translations, but only few have been hand-annotated with RRG trees. Figure 1 shows an annotated example Daakaka sentence. The basic pre-annotation model takes as input Daakaka token embeddings based on character-level LSTMs. It then labels each token with a supertag and a dependency head, which together serve as a derivation tree from which the final tree is constructed under the grammar formalism of Tree Wrapping Grammar (TWG; Kallmeyer et al., 2013). It is then shown that the accuracy of the basic model can be improved by 1) concatenating the token embeddings with similarly character-based gloss embeddings, 2) doing multiple rounds of self-training on unannotated data, and 3) using an English RRG parser (trained on substantially more gold standard data) on the translations and projecting contextualized word representations from the English parser to the Daakaka parser via unsupervised word alignments.

Proceedings of the Second Workshop on NLP Applications to Field Linguistics, pages 46–51
May 6, 2023 ©2023 Association for Computational Linguistics

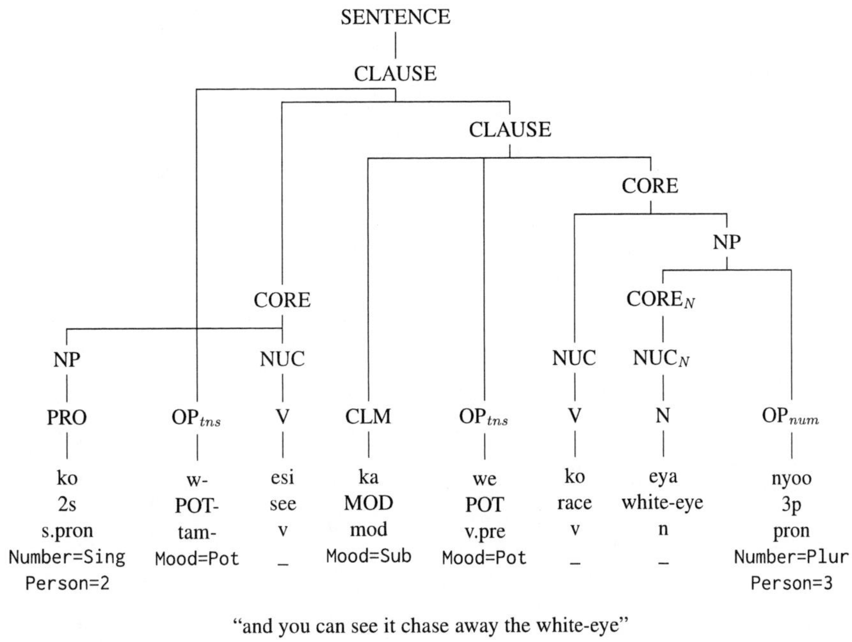

Figure 1: RRG annotation of a Daakaka sentence, with its translation. Leaf nodes contain word form, glosses, POS tags and UD features. Glosses: 2s-second person singular, 3p-third person plural, POT-potential mood marker, MOD-complementizer or modal relator. *ka* is a polysemous morpheme with different functions. It can either be a complementizer introducing subjunctive clauses, or a modal relator, which changes a directive speech act into an assertion (von Prince, 2015). Both functions appear similarly glossed in the data and were grouped together as UD feature `Mood=Sub`.

Morphological feature embeddings Adding morphological features explicitly as input on NLP tasks has mixed effects, depending on the task and quality of features. Klemen et al. (2022) show across several languages that the results on (monolingual) dependency parsing and named entity recognition improve on LSTM-based models when UD feature embeddings are added as input, while the performance on comment filtering is not affected. Manually annotated features yield better results than automatically added features. Compared to our work, their approach assumes both a rich data set in the target language and high quality of UD features. An alternative method for encoding glossed words as tensors is described by Schwartz et al. (2022), but does not provide explicit mappings from glosses to feature-value pairs.

Lemma embeddings It is standard in modern NLP systems to represent words as vectors based on word associations in unannotated running text. One such model is FastText (Bojanowski et al., 2017). Less commonly, the same kind of model is trained on lemmatized text, e.g., in Sprugnoli et al. (2019); Ehren et al. (2020).

3 Method

We build on Evang et al.'s (2022) parsing architecture, as shown in Figure 2, with our modification concerning the embedding layer. While they use the same type of character-level LSTM to generate token embeddings, part-of-speech tag embeddings, and gloss embeddings, we seek to improve performance by using a more structured representation. Glosses consist of 1) translations of lemmas to English, and 2) codes representing morphological feature values. The gloss for one token can be seen as a partial function from features to feature values, so order does not matter and different values corresponding to the same feature are mutually exclusive. For example, the gloss 2s can be represented as $\{(Number, Sing), (Person, 2)\}$. We exploit this by embedding glosses as a concatenation of feature embeddings like Klemen et al. (2022). Besides improving performance, we also aim to create a reusable compatibility layer between the glosses and Universal Dependencies (UD; de Marneffe et al., 2021), an annotation scheme commonly used in many data sets and tools. We therefore create the structured gloss embedding vectors via a mapping

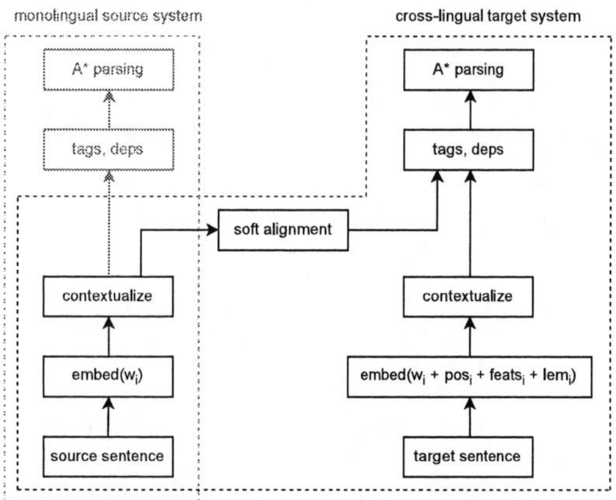

Figure 2: Architecture overview. Input on the target system includes embeddings of words, part-of-speech tags (pos), UD features, (feats) and English lemmas of target words embeddings. Words and pos tag embeddings are character-based, feats and lemmas are detailed below.

to the feature set defined by the UD annotation scheme. For the lemma translations, we exploit the fact that large quantities of text are available for English, and generate rich lemma embeddings. We now turn to the details of both contributions.

Construction of UD feature embeddings The mapping from glosses to UD features was performed with a conversion table, based on descriptions in von Prince (2015) and von Prince (2017) as well as UD guidelines. We focused on the glosses that occur in the Daakaka and Dalkalaen data (von Prince, 2013a,b). The feature `PronType` was added for pronouns, which are not particularly glossed in the data. A number of glosses were not converted to features, such as `EP` for epenthetic consonants /p/ and `ATT` for the morpheme *na*, which derives attributes from lexemes and simple phrases. Daakaka also distinguishes between three possessive classifiers glossed as `CL1`, `CL2` and `CL3` which show agreement with the lexical gender of the head noun or indicate their semantic domain (von Prince, 2015). As their function is mainly semantic and not syntactic, they were all represented as $\{(Poss, Yes)\}$. The gloss sets of both languages largely overlap; two glosses with low occurence appear only in the Dalkalaen data. We gathered 16 distinct features, 7 of which are unary (see Table 1 for an overview of the features). We did not encounter any cases where glosses on the same token mapped to conflicting values for the same feature.

Feature name	Possible values
Aspect	Inch*, Prog
Clusivity	In, Ex
Degree	Dim
Deixis*	Med, Prox, Remt
Derivation*	Nml
Mood	Ind, Irr, Pot, Sub
Number	Dual, Pauc, Plur, Sing
NumType	Card
Person	1, 2, 3
Polarity	Neg
Poss	Yes
PronType	Art, Dem, Int, Prs
Redup*	Yes
Tense	Fut, Past
Trans*	Yes
VerbType*	Aux, Cop

Table 1: Overview of UD features and possible values. * indicates that the feature or value is from a language-specific extension and not contained in the universal feature set.

For the UD feature embeddings, we follow the method described in Klemen et al. (2022). Each feature is passed through an individual embedding layer (non-present features receive a special input), yielding 3-dimensional embeddings. The final representation is a 48-dimensional vector, constructed by concatenating all feature embeddings.

Construction of lemma embeddings We use the FastText implementation of Gensim (Řehůřek and Sojka, 2010) to compute 300-dimensional lemma embeddings, trained on the lemma field of the ukWaC corpus (Baroni et al., 2009). The quality of embeddings differs across the data set. For instance, *yaapu* 'big.man' and *eya* 'white-eye' are full translations of Daakaka lemmas, however they do not appear in this form in the source corpus. The same goes for a number of names, e.g. *Simarongrong*, *Tamadu*.

4 Evaluation

We evaluate our UD feature+lemma embedding method by comparing against Evang et al.'s (2022) character-based method. We mirror their experimental setups, performing experiments across different scenarios (how much annotated seed training data is available), different amounts of self-training (adding 500 parses to the training data in each

rounds	0	1	2	3	4	5
mono, chars	67.9	69.5	70.1	70.7	70.9	70.5
mono, struct	67.9	68.5	69.5	69.5	70.2	71.2
mono, struct+lem	69.2*	$70.1_{\dagger}$	$70.8^{*}_{\dagger}$	$70.6_{\dagger}$	$71.0_{\dagger}$	$\mathbf{71.4}^{*}_{\dagger}$
cross, chars	70.2	70.7	71.7	72.2	72.4	72.2
cross, struct	70.5	71.5*	71.7	72.1	72.2	**72.5**
cross, struct+lem	70.6	71.2*	71.8	72.3	72.4	$72.3_{\dagger}$

Table 2: Daakaka test f-scores in the **very low-resource** scenario (500 training sentences) for different models (monolingual vs. cross-lingual) and different types of gloss embeddings (character-based vs. structured vs. structured + lemma embeddings. The rounds of self-training increase from left to right. The scores are averaged over five runs, except for scores marked with $_{\dagger}$ where only four successful runs were available. Results with character-based embeddings are from Evang et al. (2022). Asterisks denote significant improvement ($p \leq .05$, permutation test) over the corresponding character-based model.

rounds	0	1	2	3	4	5
mono, chars	71.9	71.5	72.4	72.9	73.4	73.3
mono, struct	71.6	71.8	72.8	73.1	72.8	**73.7**
mono, struct+lem	72.2	73.0*	**73.7***	73.3	73.2	73.3
cross, chars	73.1	73.7	74.3	74.2	74.5	74.7
cross, struct	73.3	74.2	74.3	74.6	74.6	$75.0^{*}_{\dagger}$
cross, struct+lem	73.5	73.9	74.0	74.5	74.4	**75.1***

Table 3: Daakaka test f-scores in the **low-resource** scenario (1 000 training sentences).

round), and using the monolingual vs. the cross-lingual model. We compute the overall EVALB f-score (Collins, 1997) of each model on the same test set of 196 trees (Daakaka) resp. 101 trees (Dalkalaen).

In the "very low resource scenario" (500 annotated training sentences; Table 2), we find that structured embeddings tend to improve over character-based embeddings slightly, most significantly in the early stages of self-training. We take this as an indication that structured embeddings provide the information from the start that character-based ones have to learn over mutliple rounds of self-training. We also observe that the structured models seem more stable under self-training than character-based ones: between self-training rounds 4 and 5, the two character-based models lose accuracy whereas three out of four structured models still gain accuracy. Adding lemma embeddings tends to improve over using just morphological feature embeddings.

In the "low resource scenario" (1 000 annotated training sentences; Table 3), the structured models

rounds	0	1	2	3	4	5
cross, chars	69.0	71.8	72.4	73.0	73.6	73.2
cross, struct+lem	68.9	72.1	$72.6_{\dagger}$	$73.0_{\dagger}$	$72.6_{\dagger}$	$73.1_{\dagger}$

Table 4: Dalkalaen test f-scores in the **zero-shot** scenario (no in-language training sentences, but trained on 1 840 Daakaka sentences).

are also better than the corresponding character-based ones in most cases. In the monolingual model, only the model with lemmas gives significant improvement, and only in the early rounds of self-training. In the cross-lingual model, no significant improvement is seen until the fifth round of self-training. The gain from lemma embeddings also fades. We take this as an indication that with 1 000 training trees, the cross-lingual model is already relatively strong, and it gets harder for the structured embeddings to contribute more gains. We still take this as a positive result for the structured models, as they may be able to contribute when few data or no translations are available, or self-training is impossible or impractical.

In the "zero shot" scenario (parser trained on 1 840 Daakaka trees, tested on Dalkalaen; Table 4), the structured model with lemmas is mostly on par with the character-based one, but achieves no significant improvements. We find this surprising as one would think the zero-shot model relies more strongly on feature embeddings, which are more comparable than words between both languages, and would profit more from them being structured. Further research is needed to explain this.

5 Conclusions and Future Work

We have presented an alternative way to embed data from language documentation datasets, based on structured gloss embeddings and translation lemma embeddings. We have shown that (optionally in combination with cross-linguistically projected vectors), in the context of low-resource pre-parsing for RRG treebanking, these structured embeddings can sometimes improve over character-based embeddings, or decrease the model's reliance on self-training.

Perhaps more importantly, by creating structured gloss embeddings via translation rules from interlinear glosses into UD features, we have created the first part of a compatibility layer between both types of morphosyntactic annotation, and opened the way towards morphosyntactically informed model transfer, parameter sharing, etc., between models for documented local languages and models based on existing UD treebanks. We plan to explore this option in future work. We would also like to explore sharing encoders for glossed text between more diverse sets of languages, and study the effect of the translation language on the quality of the cross-lingual word representations.

Acknowledgements

We would like to thank the anonymous reviewers for their insightful comments. This work was carried out as a part of the research project TreeGraSP[1] funded by a Consolidator Grant of the European Research Council (ERC).

References

Marco Baroni, Silvia Bernardini, Adriano Ferraresi, and Eros Zanchetta. 2009. The wacky wide web: a collection of very large linguistically processed web-crawled corpora. *Language Resources and Evaluation*, 43:209–226.

Tatiana Bladier, Kilian Evang, Valeria Generalova, Zahra Ghane, Laura Kallmeyer, Robin Möllemann, Natalia Moors, Rainer Osswald, and Simon Petitjean. 2022. RRGparbank: A parallel role and reference grammar treebank. In *Proceedings of the Thirteenth Language Resources and Evaluation Conference*, pages 4833–4841, Marseille, France. European Language Resources Association.

Piotr Bojanowski, Edouard Grave, Armand Joulin, and Tomas Mikolov. 2017. Enriching word vectors with subword information. *Transactions of the Association for Computational Linguistics*, 5:135–146.

Michael Collins. 1997. Three generative, lexicalised models for statistical parsing. In *35th Annual Meeting of the Association for Computational Linguistics and 8th Conference of the European Chapter of the Association for Computational Linguistics*, pages 16–23, Madrid, Spain. Association for Computational Linguistics.

Marie-Catherine de Marneffe, Christopher D. Manning, Joakim Nivre, and Daniel Zeman. 2021. Universal Dependencies. *Computational Linguistics*, 47(2):255–308.

Rafael Ehren, Timm Lichte, Laura Kallmeyer, and Jakub Waszczuk. 2020. Supervised disambiguation of German verbal idioms with a BiLSTM architecture. In *Proceedings of the Second Workshop on Figurative Language Processing*, pages 211–220, Online. Association for Computational Linguistics.

[1] `https://treegrasp.phil.hhu.de`

Kilian Evang, Laura Kallmeyer, Jakub Waszczuk, Kilu von Prince, Tatiana Bladier, and Simon Petitjean. 2022. Improving low-resource RRG parsing with cross-lingual self-training. In *Proceedings of the 29th International Conference on Computational Linguistics*, pages 4360–4371, Gyeongju, Republic of Korea. International Committee on Computational Linguistics.

Hildur Jónsdóttir and Anton Karl Ingason. 2020. Creating a parallel Icelandic dependency treebank from raw text to Universal Dependencies. In *Proceedings of the Twelfth Language Resources and Evaluation Conference*, pages 2924–2931, Marseille, France. European Language Resources Association.

Laura Kallmeyer, Rainer Osswald, and Robert D. Van Valin, Jr. 2013. Tree Wrapping for Role and Reference Grammar. In *Formal Grammar 2012/2013*, volume 8036 of *LNCS*, pages 175–190. Springer.

Matej Klemen, Luka Krsnik, and Marko Robnik-Šikonja. 2022. Enhancing deep neural networks with morphological information. *Natural Language Engineering*, page 1–26.

Christian Lehmann. 1982. Directions for interlinear morphemic translations. *Folia Linguistica*, 16:199–224.

Mitchell P. Marcus, Beatrice Santorini, and Mary Ann Marcinkiewicz. 1993. Building a large annotated corpus of English: The Penn Treebank. *Computational Linguistics*, 19(2):313–330.

Kilu von Prince. 2013a. *Daakaka, The Language Archive*. MPI for Psycholinguistics, Nijmegen.

Kilu von Prince. 2013b. *Dalkalaen, The Language Archive*. MPI for Psycholinguistics, Nijmegen.

Kilu von Prince. 2015. *A Grammar of Daakaka*. Mouton de Gruyter, Berlin, Boston.

Kilu von Prince. 2017. Daakaka dictionary. *Dictionaria*, (1):1–2167.

Radim Řehůřek and Petr Sojka. 2010. Software Framework for Topic Modelling with Large Corpora. In *Proceedings of the LREC 2010 Workshop on New Challenges for NLP Frameworks*, pages 45–50, Valletta, Malta. ELRA. `http://is.muni.cz/publication/884893/en`.

Lane Schwartz, Coleman Haley, and Francis Tyers. 2022. How to encode arbitrarily complex morphology in word embeddings, no corpus needed. In *Proceedings of the first workshop on NLP applications to field linguistics*, pages 64–76, Gyeongju, Republic of Korea. International Conference on Computational Linguistics.

Rachele Sprugnoli, Marco Passarotti, and Giovanni Moretti. 2019. Vir is to moderatus as mulier is to intemperans. Lemma embeddings for Latin. In *Proceedings of the Sixth Italian Conference on Computational Linguistics*, Torino, Italy. Accademia University Press.

Francis Tyers, Mariya Sheyanova, Aleksandra Martynova, Pavel Stepachev, and Konstantin Vinogorodskiy. 2018. Multi-source synthetic treebank creation for improved cross-lingual dependency parsing. In *Proceedings of the Second Workshop on Universal Dependencies (UDW 2018)*, pages 144–150, Brussels, Belgium. Association for Computational Linguistics.

Robert D. Van Valin, Jr. 2005. *Exploring the Syntax-Semantics Interface*. Cambridge University Press.

Robert D. Van Valin, Jr. and William A. Foley. 1980. Role and reference grammar. In E. A. Moravcsik and J. R. Wirth, editors, *Current approaches to syntax*, volume 13 of *Syntax and semantics*, pages 329–352. Academic Press, New York.

Approaches to Corpus Creation for Low-Resource Language Technology: the Case of Southern Kurdish and Laki

Sina Ahmadi[♠] **Zahra Azin**[♣] **Sara Belelli**[♦] **Antonios Anastasopoulos**[♠]
[♠]Department of Computer Science, George Mason University, Fairfax, VA, USA
[♣]School of Linguistics and Language Studies, Carleton University, Canada
[♦]Università degli Studi della Tuscia, Viterbo, Italy
{sahmad46,antonis}@gmu.edu, taraazin@cmail.carleton.ca, sarabelelli@gmail.com

Abstract

One of the major challenges that under-represented and endangered language communities face in language technology is the lack or paucity of language data. This is also the case of the Southern varieties of the Kurdish and Laki languages for which very limited resources are available with insubstantial progress in tools. To tackle this, we provide a few approaches that rely on the content of local news websites, a local radio station that broadcasts content in Southern Kurdish and fieldwork for Laki. In this paper, we describe some of the challenges of such under-represented languages, particularly in writing and standardization, and also, in retrieving sources of data and retro-digitizing handwritten content to create a corpus for Southern Kurdish and Laki. In addition, we study the task of language identification in light of the other variants of Kurdish and Zaza-Gorani languages.[1]

1 Introduction

Language and linguistic data play a critical role in documenting and preserving endangered and under-represented languages. Indispensable to computational methods in language technology, data also enables the development of tools and applications, such as speech recognition and machine translation, that can support the revitalization and promote the usage of such languages. As such, speakers of endangered and under-represented languages ultimately have the opportunity to share their language and cultural heritage with future generations. Despite the fascinating advances in natural language processing (NLP) in recent years, particularly in working with very limited data in low-resource setups (Hedderich et al., 2021), collecting data for endangered and less-resourced languages remains a challenging task.

[1]Datasets and models are available at https://github.com/sinaahmadi/KurdishLID

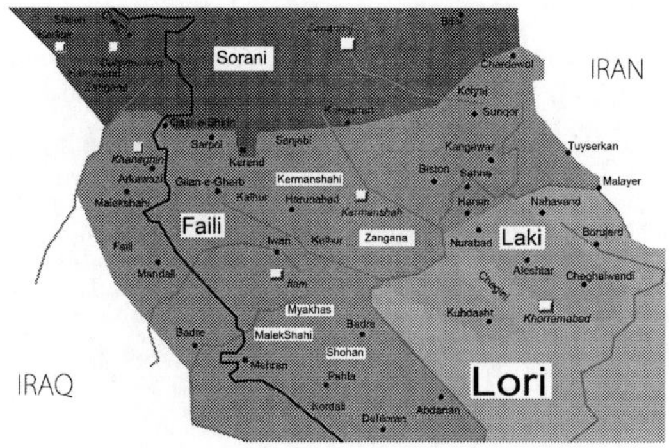

Figure 1: Territories where Central Kurdish (dark blue), Southern Kurdish (violet), Laki (pale violet) and Lori (blue) are mainly spoken. Based on Fattah (2000)

In this paper, we focus on Southern Kurdish (sdh in ISO 639-3) which is one of the main varieties of Kurdish spoken by an estimated 3.7 million speakers in the provinces of Kirmaşan, also spelled as Kermanshah, and Ilam in Iran, and across the adjoining border regions of Iraq (Eberhard et al., 2022). We also shed light on Laki (lki) spoken by a few hundred thousand speakers in the same regions (Aliakbari et al., 2015). Kurdish in general and Southern Kurdish and Laki in particular, have faced various discriminatory language policies that have led to pernicious sociolinguistic effects on language attitudes and heritage language maintenance such as the lack of children's proficiency in Southern Kurdish and limited usage of the language in writing (Sheyholislami, 2012; Tamleh et al., 2022).

As such, Southern Kurdish speakers have been facing centuries-long pressures of Persian as the only official language of Iran and the administratively dominant one, which led to various phenomena of language shift and change (Sharifi et al., 2013; Weisi, 2021; Yarahmadi, 2022). Although other varieties of Kurdish have not been immune from such policies, their larger population and strong Kurdish national and political identity be-

Proceedings of the Second Workshop on NLP Applications to Field Linguistics, pages 52–63
May 6, 2023

ing supported for a long time have been beneficial to promote the language, especially for the adjacent Central Kurdish speakers, also known as Sorani (`ckb`), in Iran and Iraq (Sheyholislami, 2010). Nevertheless, studies show that there is a positive attitude towards the Kurdish language and identity in communities of Southern Kurdish speakers as well (Rezaei and Bahrami, 2019; Sheyholislami and Sharifi, 2016).

In stark contrast to other varieties of Kurdish, particularly Northern Kurdish (`kmr`), also known as Kurmanji, and Central Kurdish, Southern Kurdish varieties and Laki have not received much attention in linguistics or computational linguistics. Moreover, for Southern Kurdish and Laki, there are relatively much fewer digital resources available, not to say near zero, and both face practical challenges in writing. On the other hand, studying these varieties *in loco*, i.e. linguistic fieldwork, is not always a viable solution given the geopolitical conditions of the region and limitations in cost and time.

Contributions This paper sheds light on creating a corpus for Southern Kurdish and Laki. We discuss possible approaches that can be taken to tackle corpus creation for under-represented and endangered languages by relying on local content creation media and also, fieldwork. Our corpus contains over 2 million tokens in Southern Kurdish and Laki. In addition to an intrinsic evaluation of the corpus, we also analyze the corpus in a qualitative way and extend our analysis to the task of language identification.

2 Southern Kurdish vs. Laki

2.1 Language Classification

Kurdish identity has been shaped by centuries of history and a strong attachment to land and culture. However, the quest for defining the Kurdish language has been a complex and challenging process, shaped by political and social factors.

Although it is difficult to define Kurdish as a homogeneous language, and it is debatable whether it should be described as a continuum of dialects, or rather as a *Sprachbund* (Jugel et al., 2014), there is broad consensus on the fact that Northern Kurdish, Central Kurdish and Southern Kurdish are the three main varieties of Kurdish as described by McCarus (2009), Edmonds (2013) and many others.

Other Iranic languages of Kurdistan, such as Zazaki (`zza`) and Gorani (`hac`) are commonly considered distinct from Kurdish even though their speakers share close cultural bonds with neighboring Kurdish communities and not rarely consider themselves as ethnically Kurds (Haig and Öpengin, 2014, cf.). That said, these two are sometimes referred to as the two other dialects of Kurdish (Eppler and Benedikt, 2017). Moreover, the classification of Laki as the southernmost variety of the Kurdish language cluster is a debated issue. On the other hand, there is full scholarly consensus on the fact that Luri (also spelled Lori, `lrc/luz`) is a Southwestern Iranic language, despite the common misconception of it being a variety of Kurdish (Anonby, 2004). Nevertheless, Lori and even more so Laki might show convergence phenomena with neighboring Southern Kurdish dialects and vice versa

In this paper, we focus on the varieties of Southern Kurdish that are spoken in the province of Kermanshah to which we refer as Kermanshahi (also spelled Kirmaşanî) and those that are spoken in Iraq. Southern Kurdish is described in the literature as a diverse group of Kurdish parlances that can be clustered into several dialect groups, among which Garrusi, Kordali, Kalhori, and Feyli as outlined by Belelli (2019, 2021). It is worth noting that here we use the term 'Feyli' as a collective denomination for some Southern Kurdish dialects spoken in border regions of Iraq and the capital Baghdad, although we recognize that the use of the term as a language label has problematic sides which cannot be further discussed here. Similarly, we also take into consideration so-called Laki-Kermanshahi varieties, which were considered as part of Southern Kurdish in (Fattah, 2000) but are perhaps better described as mixed varieties intermediate between Southern Kurdish and the Laki of northern Lorestan and eastern Ilam.

2.2 Morphosyntactic Comparison

On the differences between Northern and Central Kurdish varieties, many studies have been conducted (Matras, 2019; Esmaili and Salavati, 2013, cf.). Similarly, Belelli (2021, p. 17) lays out the major differences between Southern Kurdish and other Kurdish varieties. However, the differences between Southern Kurdish and Laki are less discussed in the literature.

Although Southern Kurdish shows morphological similarities with both Northern Kurdish and Central Kurdish, it is closer to the latter, not having

Part-of-speech			Northern Kurdish	Central Kurdish	Southern Kurdish	Laki
Noun	DEF	M	∅	*-eke*	*-ege, -eke*	*-e, -ke*
		F	∅			
		PL	∅	*-ekan*	*-egan, -ekan, -eğan, -eyle(ge)*	*-ele*
	INDF	M	*-ek*	-êk	*-î, -îg, -îk, -îğ*	*-ê, -î, -îk*
		F	*-ek*			
		PL	*-in*	*-an , -gel*	*-eyl, -gel, -ğel, -an*	*-el*
Verb		INF	*-in*	*-in*	*-in*	*-in*
		PROG	*di-*	*e- , de-*	∅*, di-, e-*	*(-e) me-*
		SBJV	*bi-*	*bi-*	*bi-*	*bi-*
Adjective		NEG	*ne-, na-*	*ne-, na-, me-*	*nye-, ne-, na-, nî-*	*nime-, ne-, nî-*
		COMP	*-tir*	*-tir*	*-tir, -tirek, -tirig*	*-tir*
		SUP	*-tirîn*	*-tirîn*	*-tirîn*	*-tirîn*

Table 1: A comparison of affixes in varieties of Kurdish and Laki. Abbreviations are according to Leipzig Glossing Rules (Comrie et al., 2008). For consistency, the Kurdified Latin script of Bedirxan is used for all. Nominal affixes are merged for variants lacking grammatical gender.

morphological markers of gender and case. Moreover, Southern Kurdish is unique within Kurdish varieties, not showing forms of tense-sensitive alignment, unlike the ergative properties of Northern and Central Kurdish. On the other hand, the differences between Southern Kurdish and Laki are less discussed in the literature, although Laki-Kermanshahi parlances have been observed to form a continuum in which the number of Laki-like features adds up proceeding from cities of Sahne towards Harsin, or rather Southern Kurdish-like traits progressively increase proceeding in the opposite direction (see Figure 1). The dialect of Harsin shows the highest level of morphological and lexical similarity with Laki "proper", while that of Sahne is the closest to Southern Kurdish.

Regarding Laki, among the typical Laki-like traits of Harsini and other Laki-Kermanshahi dialects, such as Payrawandi, Sahne'i, are the presence of phonemic /v/ as in *vitin*[2] vs Southern Kurdish *witin* 'to say', the presence of phonemic /ö/ as in *döm* 'tail' vs. Southern Kurdish *dom, dim* and variants, the form *homa* of the second person plural pronoun, a discontinuous indicative marker *=a ma-* (except Sahne having *a-* as some Southern Kurdish dialects), the use of (post)verbal particles instead of common Kurdish preverbs, such as *ör* instead of *hal* 'up', the use of different adpositional forms, such as *va* 'to, at' vs. Southern Kurdish *wa* 'to', *la/da* 'at' and the reflexive marker *wiž* as opposed to Southern Kurdish *xwa* and variants.

On the other hand, Harsini and the rest of Laki-Kermanshahi dialects have a form of the second person singular and plural verbal endings *-ī(t)/-ītin* which differs from Laki *-ī(n)/-īnān, -īnō(n)* (and of isomorphic clitic copula forms), and a form of the third person plural clitic pronoun *=yān* differing from Laki *=ān, =ō(n)*. Moreover, all Laki-Kermanshahi dialects share with Southern Kurdish the absence of forms of agentiality in the conjugation of past transitive verbs, which is otherwise a distinctive feature of Laki, as well as of Central Kurdish. Table 1 summarizes some of the frequent affixes.

2.3 Lexical Differences

Concerning Southern Kurdish and Laki, there are a series of words that are distinctive to Laki, among which *āyl* 'child', *pit* 'nose', *lam* 'stomach', *sīr* 'sated', *gojar* 'small' vs. Southern Kurdish *minal, lūt, zik, tīr, büčik/g*, respectively (Aliyari Babolghani, 2019). It must be noted that due to the sociolinguistic and geopolitical conditions, Southern Kurdish and Laki, as virtually all other regional languages, have been historically sensible to lexical borrowing from dominant languages, especially Persian and Arabic.

2.4 Writing

Although the two main scripts currently used for writing Kurdish, that is the Latin-based '*Hawar*' or '*Bedirxan*' script and the Perso-Arabic script of Central Kurdish are also adapted for writing in Southern Kurdish, with distinct graphemes such as <ۊ> (U+06CA), these scripts are not widely used among speakers who rely on a the administratively-

[2] The transcription used in this section follows (Belelli, 2021).

dominant language's writing system in practice, i.e. that of Persian or Arabic (Ahmadi et al., 2019; Filippone et al., 2022). In the same vein, Laki lacks a standard script or orthography.

Consequently, this adds to the complexity of the situation in which, a collected corpus should be written in a customized way or based on the script of a closely-related language, in this case, Central Kurdish.

3 Related Work

Although a less-resourced language, Kurdish has increasingly received attention in the past few years in language technology with tools such as the Kurdish language processing toolkit (Ahmadi, 2020b), services such as Google Translate[3] and models and benchmarks in NLP such as the FLORES-101 (Goyal et al., 2022) and NLLB (Costa-jussà et al., 2022). However, these solely include Northern and Central Kurdish but neither Southern varieties nor Laki.

Similarly, Wikipedia as an important resource to document languages is only available for Northern and Central Kurdish while Southern Kurdish and Laki along with other adjacent under-represented languages Gorani and Luri are not supported yet. Ahmadi et al. (2019) study the available lexicographical resources for Kurdish varieties and, as illustrated in Figure 2, find that among the 71 dictionaries and terminological resources available for Kurdish, Laki and Zaza-Gorani languages in electronic and printed forms, only 13.6% have content for a Southern Kurdish variety or Laki.

Previously, some linguistic aspects of Southern Kurdish have been studied such as phonology (Kord Zafaranlu Kambuziya and Sobati, 2014), typology (Dabir-Moghaddam, 2012), morphology (Belelli, 2022) and dialectology (Fattah, 2000). Belelli (2021) studies Laki and describes its complex relationship with Southern Kurdish and also documents a Laki variety by collecting a lexicon and a corpus through fieldworking.

Considering resources for language technology, Azin and Ahmadi (2021) create an electronic dictionary in Ontolex-Lemon containing 14,326 entries of varieties of Southern Kurdish in addition to Laki and Luri languages. In this resource, entries are represented in both scripts commonly used for Kurdish, even though the Latin orthography is not much used for Southern Kurdish, in addition to

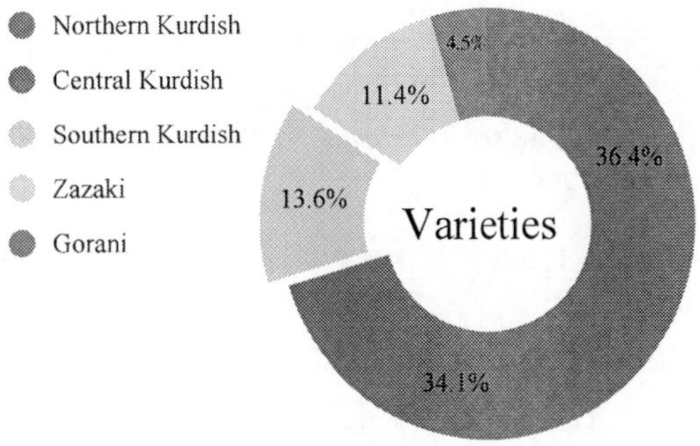

Figure 2: Percentage of the existing lexicographical resources for Kurdish varieties among which only 13.6% (<10 references) focus on Southern Kurdish and Lori.

translations in Persian and Central Kurdish. To the best of our knowledge, this dictionary is the only electronic resource for Southern Kurdish of considerable size. Similarly, Amani et al. (2021) collect audio samples for Kurdish spoken dialect recognition using radio and television contents among which 11 hours are collected for Southern Kurdish. Table 2 summarizes Kurdish and closely associated languages, along with some of the major corpora that have been previously created for them.

In addition to language documentation, corpora are crucial resources in many other applications such as language learning and teaching (Tribble, 2015), machine translation and syntactic parsing. To the best of our knowledge, no corpus of considerable size has been created for Southern Kurdish and Laki that is written in any of the two conventionalized Kurdish scripts.

4 Methodology

To remedy the lack of data for Southern Kurdish and Laki, we follow three approaches that are described in this section.

4.1 Radio Shows

In presence of local media, we resort to a local radio broadcaster in Kermanshah province (Iran) which is in majority inhabited by native speakers of Southern Kurdish. Upon our request, we could collect a set of handwritten scenarios of radio shows in Kermanshahi varieties of Southern Kurdish. The scenarios cover educational, cultural and daily topics and primarily target audiences in rural areas. Therefore, a rich native vocabulary of Southern Kurdish is employed with very few instances (if any) of code-switching to Persian or ex-

[3]https://translate.google.com

Language	639-3	Wikipedia	Common Scripts	Corpora
Northern Kurdish (Kurmanji)	kmr	ku	Latin, Central Kurdish	(Esmaili and Salavati, 2013; Ataman, 2018; Matras, 2019)
Central Kurdish (Sorani)	ckb	ckb	Central Kurdish, Latin	(Esmaili et al., 2013; Abdulrahman et al., 2019; Veisi et al., 2020; Ahmadi et al., 2020; Matras, 2019)
Southern Kurdish	sdh	-	Central Kurdish, Persian	(Fattah, 2000)
Gorani	hac	-	Central Kurdish	(Ahmadi, 2020a)
Zazaki	zza	diq	Latin	(Ahmadi, 2020a)

Table 2: Description of Kurdish varieties along with Zazaki and Gorani with some of the existing corpora and scripts ordered based on popularity. Central Kurdish script refers to the Kurdified Perso-Arabic script commonly in use in Central Kurdish.

tensive lexical borrowing from Persian.

The radio shows dataset consists of 18 scenarios written for a local radio station in the city of Kermanshah. The scenarios are written for talk shows and short comedies and broadcasted from the same radio channel. The scenarios are written for 10 to 15-minute-long programs. Most of the programs are written in the form of dialogues which makes the dataset a good fit for future discourse analysis studies.

The original scenarios were written by hand, using Persian script and orthography. We asked three Southern Kurdish speakers to type the scenarios using the Central Kurdish Perso-Arabic script. This enables us to compare the data with materials written in other varieties of Kurdish. The manually typed data were then reviewed for possible inconsistencies in the writing form used by the typists.

4.2 News Articles

In our second approach, we follow the approach of Ahmadi (2020a) to crawl content from a news website to document Southern Kurdish varieties spoken in Iraq. We found a local news website[4] that publishes news articles in a few languages including Feyli. Overall, 15,985 articles are crawled in HTML and converted to text. Following this, we carry out text preprocessing by unifying character encoding using regular expressions, cleaning the raw text by removing private information such as email addresses and text formatting and categorizing the raw text based on the topic of the article, mainly in culture, politics and Kurdistan categories.

As metadata, we provide the source, topic, title and date for the collected articles.

[4]https://shafaq.com

4.3 Fieldwork

Finally, we rely on fieldwork to document Laki and create a corpus of oral texts in the language variety spoken in Harsin city in Kermanshah province in Western Iran, belonging to the so-called Laki-Kermanshahi (or Laki-Kirmashani) dialect cluster, identified as intermediate between Southern Kurdish and Lorestani Laki (Belelli, 2021). The content of the Harsini textual corpus is typologically uniform and includes seven traditional narratives – five folktales and two anecdotes – in the form of monologues, recorded from four speakers (three female and one male) native to Harsin or the neighboring village of Parive. The texts are manually transcribed following a conventional transcription system based on the tradition of Iranian linguistics, divided into numbered annotation units, and translated into English. One of the seven texts is further interlinearized with morpheme-by-morpheme glosses.

As there is no standard writing system or orthography for Laki, using Persian script or the Kurdified scripts for Laki remains optional rather than conventional choices. This said, transliterating the corpus is possible given the consistency in the phonetic transcription.

5 Results and Analysis

In this section, we carry out an intrinsic evaluation of our corpus alongside presenting a qualitative analysis. We also extend our analysis to the task of language identification.

5.1 Quantitative Analysis

The collected data contains 16,003 documents written in varieties of Southern Kurdish and seven narratives in Laki-Kermanshahi. Table 3 presents the number of articles, tokens, types, and type characters in our collected corpus. To calculate types, i.e. unique tokens, we exclude punctuation marks, digits, and sentences tentatively flagged as code-switching, such as religious quotations in Arabic or poems in Persian. Additionally, we use regular expressions for tokenization.

Since the vocabularies of the selected varieties have much in common, we also calculate the average type length as an indicator of the morphological complexity of word forms. Although the smaller size of Kermanshahi and Laki data might not reveal much about the morphological intricacies of these varieties, the average word lengths of 6.57 of Kermanshahi and 6.45 of Laki seem to be at odds with an average length of 8.8 of types in Feyli. In comparison to the other varieties of Kurdish and Zaza-Gorani languages, Southern Kurdish appears to have longer word forms with an average length overall. According to Ahmadi (2020a), Northern and Central Kurdish have an average length of 4.8 and 5.6, respectively. Similarly, Zazaki and Gorani have an average length of 4.84 and 5.50.

We think that this remarkable difference in word length can be due to a) the orthography of the Southern Kurdish corpus, texts in Feyli in particular, b) conventions in writing multiword expressions as in بیسەروشونکریاگ (*bîserûşûnkiryag*) 'doomed' composed as بی-سەر-و-شوون-کریاگ and c) excessive concatenation of words as in گورانیچڕلوبنانی instead of گورانیچڕ لوبنانی (*goranîçirr Lubnanî*) 'Lebanese singer'. We also notice that conjunction و (*û*) 'and' and prepositions like لە (*le*) 'in' are sometimes merged with the preceding or succeeding word, as in پەلاماردەرەیلەو instead of پەلاماردەرەیلە و (*pelamardereyle û*) 'attackers and' or لەشەقامێگ instead of لە شەقامێگ (*le şeqamêk*) 'in a street'. More importantly, affixes in Southern Kurdish, as shown in Table 1, are longer than the ones in Northern and Central Kurdish resulting in a higher average word length.

Additionally, we calculate the rank-size distribution in Pewan corpus for Northern and Central Kurdish (Esmaili et al., 2013) and Zaza-Gorani corpus (Ahmadi, 2020a) along with our Southern Kurdish data (merged Kermanshahi and Feyli). According to Zipf's Law (Zipf, 1999), in such a distribution "the length of a word tends to bear an inverse relationship to its relative frequency". This is illustrated in Figure 3 where the curves for each corpus start with the most frequent words (seen

Number (#)	Kermanshahi	Feyli	Laki
articles	18	15,985	7
tokens	10,127	2,182M	6,340
types	3,248	179,208	2,074
characters	21,359	1,591M	13,378
average length	6.57	8.8	6.45

Table 3: Statistics of the collected data based on varieties of Southern Kurdish (M refers to million). The number of characters and the average length are calculated based on the types.

as dots), then words with a rank of 10 to 10000 smoothly diminish in frequency and finally, the majority of words appear at the bottom segment with lower frequencies (<10). We could not include the Laki data since this distribution requires a relatively big corpus to be valid.

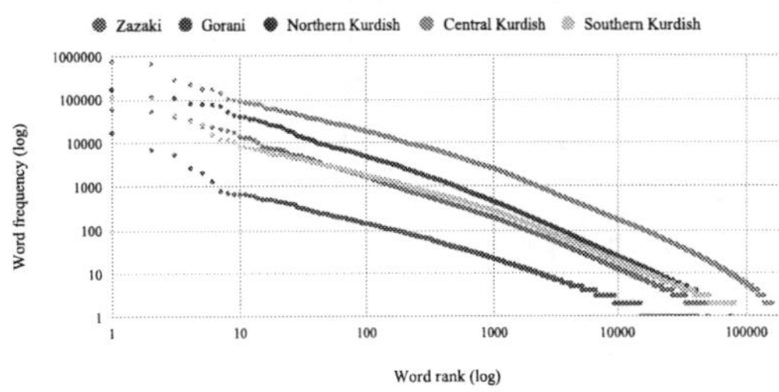

Figure 3: Zipfian distribution of Pewan corpora of Northern and Central Kurdish, a corpus of Zaza-Gorani and our corpus of Southern Kurdish (Kermanshahi and Feyli merged).

5.2 Qualitative Analysis

From a qualitative point of view, since the collected data fall into distinct textual genres, one would obviously expect differences in textual structure, lexical choices, and the level of formality. However, in the case of Southern Kurdish varieties spoken in Iraq and Iran, the most notable differences are related to the use of words classifiable as borrowings from other regional languages. Interestingly, varieties of Southern Kurdish used in Iraq tend to rely on the vocabulary of Central Kurdish as well, particularly when it comes to the terminology, while those in Iran rely more on the Persian vocabulary.

Based on the textual structure of the news articles collected for Feyli, each article has a headline that represents a concise version of the content using active voice. A collection of the headlines provides an exceptional resource for discourse analysis and further linguistic studies of the corpora. On the other hand, the data collected for Kermanshahi contains both monologues and dialogues written for radio shows. The dialogues that are written for comedy shows are in the form of two-way conversations between voice actors about social and cultural issues. The informal language used in the shows simulates real-world interactions between two speakers of Kermanshahi providing an opportunity for future conversation analysis. In the same vein, the narrative in the Laki data provides information useful to analyze folkloric stories.

Furthermore, Zipf's Law also states that the most frequent words in a language are the shorter ones due to economic factors (Sigurd et al., 2004). Table 4 provides the most frequent words in the selected corpora. Although many words among the most frequent ones have less than three characters, such as *û* 'and', *li/le/ce/de* 'in' and *bo/ara/ařā* 'for', many other words like *Kurdistan* and *Iraq* appear frequently indicating the topics of the texts and also, the bias and a lack of diversity in domains. This is also affected by the orthography of the language as postpositions like *ra* in Zazaki and *de* in Northern Kurdish appear frequently, while the equivalent ones in Central Kurdish as *da* and *ewe* don't appear so. Nevertheless, the most frequent words in Laki data show elements from the narratives such as *muše* 'IND-SAY.PRS-3SG'.

Despite sharing many linguistic features, the variations between Southern Kurdish varieties and Laki-Kermanshahi are not negligible. As previously discussed, the scarcity of language data and a lack of a writing system for this branch of Kurdish are among the reasons we still do not have a clear picture of the extant variation in the written forms of its sub-varieties.

5.3 Language Identification

Language identification or detection is the task of detecting the language in which a sentence is written. This task is used in many downstream applications in NLP such as sentiment analysis (Vilares et al., 2017), text summarization (Kanapala et al., 2019), code-mixed detection in multilingual documents and on the Web (Bhargava et al., 2016) and machine translation (Sefara et al., 2021). Although language identification has been previously addressed for some of the varieties of Kurdish such as Central Kurdish (Malmasi, 2016), this task is not explored considering all Kurdish varieties.

In addition to the sentences that we extract from our corpus, we collect 3000 sentences for other varieties of Kurdish from the available corpora as follows: Central Kurdish in Perso-Arabic script and Northern Kurdish in Latin script both from the Pewan corpus (Esmaili et al., 2013), Central Kurdish in Latin script from the Wergor corpus (Ahmadi, 2019) and, Zazaki and Gorani sentences from Ahmadi (2020a). Given that types of Northern Kurdish are also written in Perso-Arabic script, particularly in Iraqi Kurdistan, we also collect sentences from online forums and websites that publish in Northern Kurdish written in the Perso-Arabic script. Moreover, we noticed that the script and orthography that is used for Zazaki on its dedicated Wikipedia page[5] is different from the script which is used in Ahmadi (2020a)'s corpus; the latter entirely corresponds to the '*Hawar*' or '*Bedirxan*' system conventionalized for Northern Kurdish (Littell et al., 2016) while the former is influenced by the Turkish Latin script. We did not include the Laki data in this task as the writing system for Laki is yet to be defined in practice. To further diversify the task, we include sentences in Arabic, Persian and Turkish from the Tatoeba datasets as well.[6]

As the baseline system, we evaluate the pre-trained language identifier of fastText (Bojanowski et al., 2017) which can recognize 176 languages including Northern Kurdish, Central Kurdish and Zazaki, respectively with `kmr`, `ckb` and `diq` identifiers. In addition, we train our classifiers where the target classes, i.e. label of the language, include the code of the script, e.g. `ckbarab` and `ckblatn` are used to differentiate between Central Kurdish (`ckb`) text written in the Perso-Arabic and Latin scripts, respectively. Similarly, we consider a classification scenario where the labels are aggregated based on the language code only. As such, we train our model using fastText with the following hyper-parameters: 25 epochs, word vectors of size 64, a minimum and maximum length of char n-gram of 2 to 6, a learning rate of 1.0 and hierarchical softmax as the loss function.

Table 5 presents our experimental results of language identification for the selected varieties and scripts. Although the pretrained fastText model–`lid.176` performs poorly, chiefly due to the fact that it has not been trained on our target languages. The results indicate that our trained model per-

[5]https://diq.wikipedia.org

[6]https://tatoeba.org

Northern Kurdish	Central Kurdish	Southern Kurdish		Laki	Gorani	Zazaki
		Feyli	Kermanshahi			
û (and)	*le* (from, in)	*e* (is)	*û* (and)	*muše* (IND-SAY.PRS-3SG)	*û* (and)	*de* (in)
ku (that)	*û* (and)	*û* (and)	*we* (and)	*ī* (this, these)	*ce* (in)	*û* (and)
li (from, in)	*bo* (for)	*ki* (that)	*le* (in)	*ye* (a, an)	*be* (to, with)	*ke* (that)
bi (with, to)	*be* (with, to)	*we* (and)	*abadî* (village)	*ařā* (for)	*ke* (that)	*ra*
di (in)	*ke* (that)	*era* (for)	*naw* (in; name)	*va* (to)	*pey* (for)	*bi* (with)
ji (from)	*ew* (that)	*ew* (that)	*wegerd* (with)	*maču* (IND-GO.PRS-3SG)	*y*	*ma* (we)
de	*Kurdistan*	*kird* (ind-do.pst-3sg)	*ta* (until)	*ya* (this, this one)	*ta* (until)	*xo* (self)
jî (too)	*Iraq*	wit (IND-SAY.PST-3SG)	*ê* (this)	*a* (yes; that)	*î* (this)	*zî* (too)
Kurdistanê	*em* (this)	*herêm* (region, region of)	*î* (this)	*make* (IND-DO.PRS-3SG)	*Kurdistanî*	*yê*
Iraqê	*herêmî* (region of)	*Kurdistan*	*weşûn* (after)	*mi* (me, mine)	*her* (each)	*mi* (my)
herêma (region of)	*serokî* (president of)	*ta* (until)	*bün* (IND-BE.PST-3PL)	*nām* (name)	*Turkyay* (Turkey)	*o* (that, it)

Table 4: The 10 most frequent words in Northern and Central Kurdish and Zaza-Gorani corpora along with our collected data in Southern Kurdish and Laki-Kermanshahi. In addition to frequent function words like prepositions and conjunctions, many words appear related to the topic of the texts, such as *Kurdistan* and *Iraq*.

Measure	`lid.176`	Our model		
		language code	language & script code	SDH-unconventional
Precision	0.0552	0.969	0.9638	0.25
Recall	0.0674	0.971	0.9636	0.126
F_1	0.06	**0.97**	0.9634	0.168

Table 5: Results of language identification with and without the script code (`arab,latn`) included in the label for classification. Unconventional refers to the identification of Southern Krudish text written in Persian script rather than Kurdish. Our models outperform the baseline (pretrained fastText). Measures are computed using the arithmetic mean (also known as macro or unweighted mean).

forms well in both setups where the language code is only provided for the classification task as in `ckb` and also, in the case where the script code is provided as in `ckbarab`. We also evaluate our model on the Southern Kurdish data that is written in the Persian script and orthography prior to being harmonized with the Central Kurdish Perso-Arabic script. An F_1 measure of 0.168 reflects the difficulty of this task in a noisy setup as such. A few examples with predictions and heatmaps of the predictions are provided in Table A.1 and Figure A.1.

6 Conclusion

Data in general, and corpora in particular, provide a foundation for the preservation and promotion of endangered and under-represented languages in language technology. In this paper, we discuss three approaches for data collection and corpus creation of low-resourced and under-represented languages, namely Southern Kurdish varieties spoken in Kermanshah province (Iran) and Feyli varieties spoken in Iraq. While the Kermanshahi dataset has been collected from a local radio station and by crawling a news website, we collected data for Laki by fieldwork, which despite considerable challenges, seems to be the only solution for a language with near zero online presence. Our approaches can be adopted by other under-represented languages with limited data and without the possibility of fieldwork. We finally provide a brief analysis from quantitative and qualitative perspectives along with the evaluation of language identification for Kurdish and Zaza-Gorani languages with different scripts. Our model can be beneficial to detect texts and collecting more data.

Regarding future work, a data-driven approach can be explored to shed light on the various linguistic differences among the selected languages and varieties. Moreover, as our target languages have been under the threat of linguistic assimilation (Hasanpoor, 1999), particularly through lexical borrowing from Persian, Arabic and Turkish, a new problem transpires which is to determine lexical borrowing. We believe that lexical borrowing detection (Miller et al., 2020) can be further studied in the future thanks to our data. The collected corpora can pave the way for further developments in language technology and cross-lingual studies. Finally, annotating these corpora for other tasks, particularly part-of-speech tagging and named entity recognition can be addressed in the future.

7 Limitations

One of the major limitations of the current study is the small size of the collected data with Kermanshahi and Laki having less than 20,000 tokens. Therefore, it is necessary to extend the current data to be able to analyze the languages based on the corpus in a meaningful way (Davies, 2018). The qualitative analysis could be extended to examine the sentence and word length preferences based on the type of text and also, the variety and language.

In order to harmonize the data in Laki and make them comparable with the rest of the Southern Kurdish corpus, transliteration of the Laki corpus is required. However, this requires more discussions among the concerned language community to employ a writing system as the conventional one.

Acknowledgments

Sina Ahmadi and Antonios Anastasopoulos are generously supported by the National Science Foundation under DEL/DLI award BCS-2109578. The authors are also thankful to the anonymous reviewers.

References

Roshna Abdulrahman, Hossein Hassani, and Sina Ahmadi. 2019. Developing a Fine-grained Corpus for a Less-resourced Language: the case of Kurdish. In *Proceedings of the 2019 Workshop on Widening NLP*, pages 106–109.

Sina Ahmadi. 2019. A Rule-Based Kurdish Text Transliteration System. *ACM Trans. Asian Low Resour. Lang. Inf. Process.*, 18(2):18:1–18:8.

Sina Ahmadi. 2020a. Building a Corpus for the Zaza-Gorani Language Family. In *Proceedings of the 7th Workshop on NLP for Similar Languages, Varieties and Dialects, VarDial@COLING 2020, Barcelona, Spain (Online), December 13, 2020*, pages 70–78. International Committee on Computational Linguistics (ICCL).

Sina Ahmadi. 2020b. KLPT – Kurdish language processing toolkit. In *Proceedings of Second Workshop for NLP Open Source Software (NLP-OSS)*, pages 72–84, Online. Association for Computational Linguistics.

Sina Ahmadi, Hossein Hassani, and Daban Q. Jaff. 2020. Leveraging Multilingual News Websites for Building a Kurdish Parallel Corpus. *CoRR*, abs/2010.01554.

Sina Ahmadi, Hossein Hassani, and John P McCrae. 2019. Towards electronic lexicography for the Kurdish language. In *Proceedings of the sixth biennial conference on electronic lexicography (eLex)*. eLex 2019.

Mohammad Aliakbari, Mojtaba Gheitasi, and Erik Anonby. 2015. On language distribution in Ilam province, Iran. *Iranian studies*, 48(6):835–850.

Salman Aliyari Babolghani. 2019. Is Lakī a Kurdish dialect. *Iranian studies in honour of Adriano V. Rossi*, pages 3–20.

Arash Amani, Mohammad Mohammadamini, and Hadi Veisi. 2021. Kurdish Spoken Dialect Recognition Using X-Vector Speaker Embedding. In *Speech and Computer: 23rd International Conference, SPECOM 2021, St. Petersburg, Russia, September 27–30, 2021, Proceedings 23*, pages 50–57. Springer.

Erik Anonby. 2004. Kurdish or Luri. *Laki's disputed identity in the Luristan province of Iran. Kurdische Studien*, 4(5):7–22.

Duygu Ataman. 2018. Bianet: A parallel news corpus in Turkish, Kurdish and English. *arXiv preprint arXiv:1805.05095*.

Zahra Azin and Sina Ahmadi. 2021. Creating an Electronic Lexicon for the Under-resourced Southern Varieties of Kurdish Language. *Proceedings of Seventh Biennial Conference on Electronic Lexicography (eLex 2021)*.

Sara Belelli. 2019. Towards a dialectology of Southern Kurdish: Where to begin. *Current issues in Kurdish linguistics*, 1:73.

Sara Belelli. 2021. *The Laki variety of Harsin : grammar, texts, lexicon.* University of Bamberg Press, Bamberg.

Sara Belelli. 2022. A Cross-Dialect Account of Kurdish Past Tense Categories, with Special Reference to Southern Kurdish. In *Structural and Typological Variation in the Dialects of Kurdish*, pages 239–290. Springer.

Rupal Bhargava, Yashvardhan Sharma, and Shubham Sharma. 2016. Sentiment analysis for mixed script Indic sentences. In *2016 International Conference on Advances in Computing, Communications and Informatics, ICACCI 2016, Jaipur, India, September 21-24, 2016*, pages 524–529. IEEE.

Piotr Bojanowski, Edouard Grave, Armand Joulin, and Tomas Mikolov. 2017. Enriching word vectors with subword information. *Transactions of the association for computational linguistics*, 5:135–146.

Bernard Comrie, Martin Haspelmath, and Balthasar Bickel. 2008. The Leipzig Glossing Rules: Conventions for interlinear morpheme-by-morpheme glosses. *Department of Linguistics of the Max Planck Institute for Evolutionary Anthropology & the Department of Linguistics of the University of Leipzig. Retrieved January*, 28:2010.

Marta R. Costa-jussà, James Cross, Onur Çelebi, Maha Elbayad, Kenneth Heafield, Kevin Heffernan, Elahe Kalbassi, Janice Lam, Daniel Licht, Jean Maillard, Anna Sun, Skyler Wang, Guillaume Wenzek, Al Youngblood, Bapi Akula, Loïc Barrault, Gabriel Mejia Gonzalez, Prangthip Hansanti, John Hoffman, Semarley Jarrett, Kaushik Ram Sadagopan, Dirk Rowe, Shannon Spruit, Chau Tran, Pierre Andrews, Necip Fazil Ayan, Shruti Bhosale, Sergey Edunov, Angela Fan, Cynthia Gao, Vedanuj Goswami, Francisco Guzmán, Philipp Koehn, Alexandre Mourachko, Christophe Ropers, Safiyyah Saleem, Holger Schwenk, and Jeff Wang. 2022. No Language Left Behind: Scaling Human-Centered Machine Translation. *CoRR*, abs/2207.04672.

Mohammad Dabir-Moghaddam. 2012. Linguistic typology: An Iranian perspective. *Journal of Universal Language*, 13(1):31–70.

Mark Davies. 2018. Corpus-based studies of lexical and semantic variation: The importance of both corpus size and corpus design. In *From data to evidence in English language research*, pages 66–87. Brill.

David M Eberhard, Gary F Simons, and Charles D Fennig. 2022. Ethnologue: Languages of the world. *Dallas: SIL International.*

Alexander Johannes Edmonds. 2013. The Dialects of Kurdish. *Ruprecht-Karls-Universität Heidelberg.*

Eva Eppler and Josef Benedikt. 2017. A perceptual dialectological approach to linguistic variation and spatial analysis of Kurdish varieties. *Journal of Linguistic Geography*, 5(2):109–130.

Kyumars Sheykh Esmaili, Donya Eliassi, Shahin Salavati, Purya Aliabadi, Asrin Mohammadi, Somayeh Yosefi, and Shownem Hakimi. 2013. Building a test collection for Sorani Kurdish. In *2013 ACS International Conference on Computer Systems and Applications (AICCSA)*, pages 1–7. IEEE.

Kyumars Sheykh Esmaili and Shahin Salavati. 2013. Sorani Kurdish versus Kurmanji Kurdish: An empirical comparison. In *Proceedings of the 51st Annual Meeting of the Association for Computational Linguistics (Volume 2: Short Papers)*, volume 2, pages 300–305.

Ismail Kamandar Fattah. 2000. *Les dialectes kurdes méridionaux: Étude linguistique et dialectologique (Acta Iranica 37).* Peeters, Leuven.

Ela Filippone, Sara Belelli, and Matteo De Chiara. 2022. *Divisi dalla "penna" e dalla "spada": la codifica delle grafie kurde, dai fratelli Bedir Khan e Taufiq Wahby al kurdo me-ridionale* (divided by the "pen" and the "sword": codifying kurdish orthographies, from the bedir khan brothers and taufiq wahby to southern kurdish). pages 93–106.

Naman Goyal, Cynthia Gao, Vishrav Chaudhary, Peng-Jen Chen, Guillaume Wenzek, Da Ju, Sanjana Krishnan, Marc'Aurelio Ranzato, Francisco Guzmán, and Angela Fan. 2022. The Flores-101 Evaluation Benchmark for Low-Resource and Multilingual Machine Translation. *Trans. Assoc. Comput. Linguistics*, 10:522–538.

Geoffrey Haig and Ergin Öpengin. 2014. Introduction to Special Issue-Kurdish: A critical research overview. *Kurdish studies*, 2(2):99–122.

Jafar Hasanpoor. 1999. *A study of European, Persian and Arabic loans in standard Sorani.* Uppsala University.

Michael A. Hedderich, Lukas Lange, Heike Adel, Jannik Strötgen, and Dietrich Klakow. 2021. A survey on recent approaches for natural language processing in low-resource scenarios. In *Proceedings of the 2021 Conference of the North American Chapter of the Association for Computational Linguistics: Human Language Technologies*, pages 2545–2568, Online. Association for Computational Linguistics.

Thomas Jugel et al. 2014. On the linguistic history of Kurdish. *Kurdish Studies*, 2(2):123–142.

Ambedkar Kanapala, Sukomal Pal, and Rajendra Pamula. 2019. Text summarization from legal documents: a survey. *Artif. Intell. Rev.*, 51(3):371–402.

Aliyeh Kord Zafaranlu Kambuziya and Elham Sobati. 2014. Phonological processes of consonants in Kalhori Kurdish dialect. *Language Related Research*, 5(1):191–222.

Patrick Littell, David R Mortensen, Kartik Goyal, Chris Dyer, and Lori Levin. 2016. Bridge-language capitalization inference in Western Iranian: Sorani, Kurmanji, Zazaki, and Tajik. In *Proceedings of the Tenth International Conference on Language Resources and Evaluation (LREC'16)*, pages 3318–3324.

Shervin Malmasi. 2016. Subdialectal differences in Sorani Kurdish. In *Proceedings of the third workshop on nlp for similar languages, varieties and dialects (vardial3)*, pages 89–96.

Yaron Matras. 2019. Revisiting Kurdish dialect geography: findings from the Manchester database. *Current issues in Kurdish linguistics*, 1:225.

Ernest N. McCarus. 2009. Kurdish. *Windfuhr, Gernot. ed. The Iranian languages. London: Routledge*, 1:587–633.

John E Miller, Tiago Tresoldi, Roberto Zariquiey, César A Beltrán Castañón, Natalia Morozova, and Johann-Mattis List. 2020. Using lexical language models to detect borrowings in monolingual wordlists. *Plos one*, 15(12):e0242709.

Saeed Rezaei and Ava Bahrami. 2019. Attitudes toward Kurdish in the City of Ilam in Iran. *The sociolinguistics of Iran's languages at home and abroad: The case of Persian, Azerbaijani, and Kurdish*, pages 77–106.

Tshephisho J. Sefara, Skhumbuzo G. Zwane, Nelisiwe Gama, Hlawulani Sibisi, Phillemon N. Senoamadi, and Vukosi Marivate. 2021. Transformer-based Machine Translation for Low-resourced Languages embedded with Language Identification. In *Conference on Information Communications Technology and Society, ICTAS 2021, Virtual Event / Durban, South Africa, March 10-11, 2021*, pages 127–132. IEEE.

Shahla Sharifi, Mahmoud Elyasi, and Amir Karimi Pour. 2013. The Analysis of Language Change in The Kurdish Narratives Produced by 60 Kurdish-Persian Bilinguals. *Asian Journal of Social Sciences and Humanities*, 2.

Jaffer Sheyholislami. 2010. Identity, language, and new media: The Kurdish case. *Language policy*, 9(4).

Jaffer Sheyholislami. 2012. Kurdish in Iran: A case of restricted and controlled tolerance. *International Journal of the Sociology of Language*, 2012(217):19–47.

Jaffer Sheyholislami and Amir Sharifi. 2016. "It is the hardest to keep": Kurdish as a heritage language in the United States. *International Journal of the Sociology of Language*, 2016(237):75–98.

Bengt Sigurd, Mats Eeg-Olofsson, and Joost Van Weijer. 2004. Word length, sentence length and frequency–Zipf revisited. *Studia linguistica*, 58(1):37–52.

Hadis Tamleh, Saeed Rezaei, and Nettie Boivin. 2022. Family language policy among Kurdish–Persian speaking families in Kermanshah, Iran. *Multilingua*, 41(6):743–767.

Christopher Tribble. 2015. Teaching and language corpora. *Multiple affordances of language corpora for data-driven learning*, 69:37–62.

Hadi Veisi, Mohammad MohammadAmini, and Hawre Hosseini. 2020. Toward Kurdish language processing: Experiments in collecting and processing the AsoSoft text corpus. *Digital Scholarship in the Humanities*, 35(1):176–193.

David Vilares, Miguel A. Alonso, and Carlos Gómez-Rodríguez. 2017. Supervised sentiment analysis in multilingual environments. *Inf. Process. Manag.*, 53(3):595–607.

Hiwa Weisi. 2021. Language dominance and shift among Kalhuri Kurdish speakers in the multilingual context of Iran: Linguistic suicide or linguicide? *Language Problems and Language Planning*, 45(1):56–79.

Javad Yarahmadi. 2022. Language change among Kalhuri Kurdish speakers in Iran: A gain or in vain? *Pragmatics and Society*, 13(2):322–340.

G.K. Zipf. 1999. *The Psycho-Biology of Language: An Introduction to Dynamic Philology*. Cognitive psychology]. Routledge.

Language	Script	Prediction		Sentence
		`lid.176`	Our's	
Northern Kurdish	Bedirxan	KU	KU	Evî jêderî got, ku gundên Reşave, û Kukerê, kevtin ber evê topbarankirinê
Northern Kurdish	Central Kurdish	CKB	KU	نێزیکی ٦ هەیڤایە کێشە د ناڤبەرا هێزێن سیاسی یێن سەرکەفتی د هەلبژارتن بەردەوامە
Central Kurdish	Central Kurdish	CKB	CKB	هەروەها ڕاشیگەیاند، لەتەواوی نەخۆشخانەکاندا برینداران چارەسەریان وەرگرتووە
Central Kurdish	Bedirxan	KU	CKB	Parlemanî Turkya dengî be paketî hawdengîy yekêtê Ewrûpa da.
Southern Kurdish (Feyli)	Central Kurdish	CKB	SDH	نرخ تەڵای بیگانە و عراقی لە بازاڕە ناوخۆیەکان ئەرا ئمڕوو دووشەممە داوەزیا
Southern Kurdish (Kermanshahi)	Central Kurdish	CKB	SDH	باشد ئاقا ئشتبا کردیم، وە خاتر وەزن قافیە شێعرەگە وەتم، بوەخشی گەپمان قسەس
Southern Kurdish (Kermanshahi)	Persian	FA	FA	امیدواریم له هر جای استان عزیزمان کرماشان، دەنگمای شنوین، دلخوەش بیون
Zazaki	Bedirxan	KU	ZZA	Şima seba îadeyê heqanê şarê Dêrsimî û qedînayîşê polîtîkayanê teda
Zazaki	Wikipedia	DIQ	ZZA	Agariyaki yew zıwanê Hindıstaniyo. Aidê gruba Zıwanê Mundayo.
Gorani	Central Kurdish	CKB	HAC	ئازاڎ و سەربەوێ و شایان و نموونە بۆ و هەرپاسە داراو پلە وپایەی بەرزی کۆمەڵایەتی

Table A.1: A few examples in the selected languages along with the predictions of fastText's pretrained models (`lid.176`) in comparison to those of our model trained using fastText on our collected data. Northern Kurdish (KU), Central Kurdish (CKB) and Southern Kurdish (SDH) are used along with Gorani (HAC) and Zazaki (ZZA) in various scripts. DIQ refers to the script that is used for Zazaki on Wikipedia.

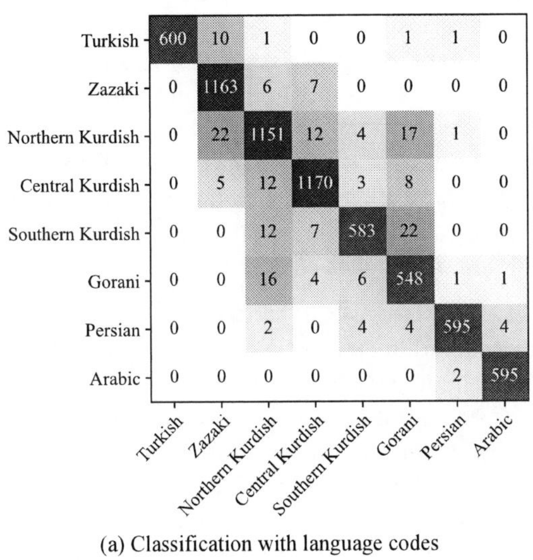

(a) Classification with language codes

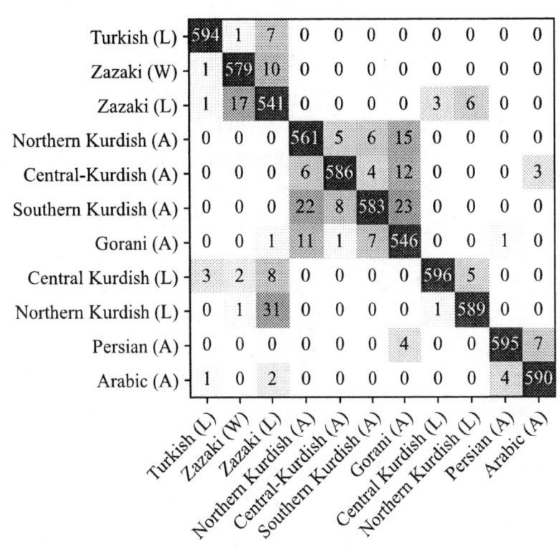

(b) Classification with language and script codes

Figure A.1: Language identification of Kurdish varieties and Zaza-Gorani when considering the script as a label (to the right) and without the script (to the left). Script codes are shown as L, A and W for Latin, Arabic and Zazaki Wikipedia. The number of classifications is annotated. Horizontal and vertical axes refer to reference labels and model predictions, respectively.

AraDiaWER: An Explainable Metric For Dialectical Arabic ASR

Abdulwahab Sahyoun and **Shady Shehata***
Mohamed bin Zayed University of Artificial Intelligence
Abu Dhabi, United Arab Emirates
abdulwahab.sahyoun@mbzuai.ac.ae, shady.shehata@mbzuai.ac.ae

Abstract

Linguistic variability poses a challenge to many modern ASR systems, particularly Dialectical Arabic (DA) ASR systems dealing with low-resource dialects and resulting morphological and orthographic variations in text and speech. Traditional evaluation metrics such as the word error rate (WER) inadequately capture these complexities, leading to an incomplete assessment of DA ASR performance. We propose AraDiaWER, an ASR evaluation metric for Dialectical Arabic (DA) speech recognition systems, focused on the Egyptian dialect. AraDiaWER uses language model embeddings for the syntactic and semantic aspects of ASR errors to identify their root cause, not captured by traditional WER. MiniLM generates the semantic score, capturing contextual differences between reference and predicted transcripts. CAMeLBERT-Mix assigns morphological and lexical tags using a fuzzy matching algorithm to calculate the syntactic score. Our experiments validate the effectiveness of AraDiaWER. By incorporating language model embeddings, AraDiaWER enables a more interpretable evaluation, allowing us to improve DA ASR systems. We position the proposed metric as a complementary tool to WER, capturing syntactic and semantic features not represented by WER. Additionally, we use UMAP analysis to observe the quality of ASR embeddings in the proposed evaluation framework.

1 Introduction

State-of-the-art (SoTA) ASR systems such as Wav2Vec2 XLSR-53 (Baevski et al., 2020), HuBERT (Hsu et al., 2021), and Whisper (Radford et al., 2022) are designed to perform on a wide range of languages, including Arabic speech. To benchmark these models, WER and character error rate (CER) metrics are used to calculate the number of words inserted, substituted, and deleted in transcribed speech. WER then calculates the error percentage by dividing by the total number of words in the predicted transcript. This yields an error rate that quantifies a basic comparison without any language-specific analysis. WER is not designed to consider any form of syntactical or semantic differences in the reference transcript and the predicted transcript, but rather to compare them word by word. This form of calculation poses a gap in the evaluation methodology used for benchmarking ASR systems that deal with multiple languages and dialects of the same language, particularly Dialectical Arabic (DA), which imposes a multitude of morphological and orthographic variations. In the evaluation landscape, metrics present themselves as the source of truth for the quantities they report. However, most metrics used in research today do not give researchers enough insight into the reasoning behind the results and the methodologies used within the metric. This poses a critical issue for explaining results when a system deals with a multitude of morphological variations in speech. To improve the explainability of the results, our research work focuses on proposing a transparent method that provides a new metric named AraDiaWER that is based on WER with a new explainable identity, allowing the metric to report additional semantic and syntactic scores.

It is well established that WER could be used as a benchmark metric for most speech recognition tasks, and in most languages, it works fairly well. However, the challenges imposed by synthetic languages and the lack of syntactic and semantic context of WER, as shown in (Kim et al., 2021), have required researchers to explore methods designed around the language itself. (Ali et al., 2015, 2017; Ali and Renals, 2018; Ali et al., 2019; Ali and Renals, 2020) are five SoTA systems that propose supervised, unsupervised, and objective-based evaluation of Arabic ASR systems. SemDist (Kim et al., 2021), FLORES (Goyal et al., 2021), and the study of lexical distance (Kwaik et al., 2018) provide a

*Corresponding author

Proceedings of the Second Workshop on NLP Applications to Field Linguistics, pages 64–73
May 6, 2023

semantic distance component combined with NER tags and intent recognition to improve the evaluation of ASR systems. Our proposed AraDiaWER metric incorporates semantic and syntactic scoring, fluency scoring, and a UMAP analysis to better explain the performance of DA ASR, while also keeping the traditional metrics (*i.e.,* WER) intact and available for benchmarking purposes.

2 AraDiaWER Methodology

To introduce additional syntactic and semantic variances to the existing WER metric and enhance its explainability, we proposed the AraDiaWER metric. We used a weighted sum approach to capture more differences in utterances while maintaining the integrity and distribution of WER.

We designed AraDiaWER to depend on the semantic and syntactic weight generated by other models through a factor we call the error weight or W_{err}. The portable dependency on other LMs for the semantic and syntactic scores provides flexibility for other researchers to improve AraDiaWER or adjust the SoTA models used for the syntactic and semantic components to their specific use cases.

To assess the performance of the proposed metric, we fine-tuned a Wav2Vec2-based model with a Connectionist Temporal Classification scorer on a large Arabic speech dataset with more than ten dialects. We compared the performance of the fine-tuned model with five other state-of-the-art ASR systems.

2.1 Datasets

This work focuses on evaluating the performance of Dialectical Arabic (DA) ASR systems, which must deal with low-resource dialects and resulting morphological and orthographic variations in text and speech. To evaluate the AraDiaWER metric, datasets that represent the dialectical variations of Arabic, particularly Egyptian dialects are required. We evaluate various ASR systems, including those developed by AALTO (Smit et al., 2017), MIT (Najafian et al., 2017), JHU (Manohar et al., 2017), BUT (Vesely et al., 2017), Mo, and NDSC, and the TDNN-based ASR system in (Ali et al., 2014). All evaluated models vary in their specific implementations but are primarily based on TDNN and LSTM architectures, which are considered hybrid ASR systems. These systems rely on an acoustic model, language model, and lexicons or phonemes to effectively process and recognize dialectal variations

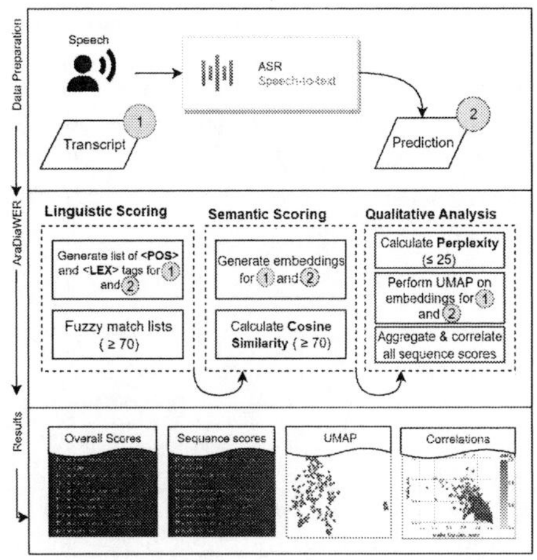

Figure 1: Illustration of AraDiaWER end-to-end approach. The main inputs are the references and predictions.

within Arabic speech.

Our experiments use several datasets that are specifically designed for Arabic speech recognition, including the MGB-3 dataset, which contains 1,000 Egyptian speech samples in the adaptation set and 2,058 samples in the development set. We also use the Arabic subset in FLEURS, which contains 428 samples of Egyptian speech from 180 unique speakers. These datasets were chosen because they represent the specific dialectical variations of Arabic that we aim to evaluate with our metric.

Moreover, we evaluate several SoTA ASR systems, including our fine-tuned AraDia-CTC model, Whisper, Wav2Vec2 XLSR-53, and HuBERT, on the MGB3 test set with 297 samples. The chosen SoTA ASR systems represent the current state of the art in Arabic speech recognition and provide a benchmark for the AraDiaWER metric.

2.2 Metric End-to-End Approach

AraDiaWER metric is designed to add explainability to the existing WER metric by incorporating additional syntactic and semantic variances. To achieve this, our framework includes three pipelines: data loading, prediction, and evaluation. The data loading pipeline converts speech audio data into feature tensors, which are then used by the prediction pipeline to transcribe the speech data into text using any ASR system (e.g., Whisper, Wav2Vec2). Once the prediction transcripts are generated, the evaluation pipeline uses two language models to determine the syntactic match and semantic similarity between the reference and

Table 1: Ablation of all syntactic (syntax) tags for the AALTO ASR system using the MGB3 evaluation set.

Configuration	AraDiaWER	Syntactic Score	Semantic Score	Error Weight
syntax7 (pos,lex,prc0,prc1,prc2,prc3,enc0)	0.268	0.863	0.925	0.559
syntax6 (pos,lex,prc0,prc1,prc2,prc3)	**0.268**	**0.863**	**0.925**	**0.559**
syntax5 (pos,lex,prc0,prc1,prc2)	0.268	0.855	0.925	0.561
syntax4 (pos,lex,prc0,prc1)	0.270	0.853	0.925	0.562
syntax3 (pos,lex,prc0)	0.269	0.848	0.925	0.564
syntax2 (pos,lex)	0.271	0.837	0.925	0.567
syntax1 (pos)	0.270	0.844	0.925	0.565

Table 2: Ablation of all syntactic (syntax) tags for the TDNN ASR system using the MGB3 development set.

Configuration	AraDiaWER	Syntactic Score	Semantic Score	Error Weight
syntax7 (pos,lex,prc0,prc1,prc2,prc3,enc0)	0.604	0.708	0.833	0.648
syntax6 (pos,lex,prc0,prc1,prc2,prc3)	**0.604**	**0.708**	**0.833**	**0.648**
syntax5 (pos,lex,prc0,prc1,prc2)	0.605	0.698	0.833	0.653
syntax4 (pos,lex,prc0,prc1)	0.606	0.694	0.833	0.654
syntax3 (pos,lex,prc0)	0.607	0.685	0.833	0.658
syntax2 (pos,lex)	0.611	0.665	0.833	0.670
syntax1 (pos)	0.607	0.690	0.833	0.656

prediction transcripts. These two language models act as the basis for the semantic and syntactic components of the AraDiaWER metric. Figure 1 illustrates the end-to-end AraDiaWER process, highlighting the significance of the syntactic and semantic components in improving the evaluation of DA ASR systems.

The explainability of AraDiaWER with respect to the correlation between substitution/insertion/deletion and semantic and syntactic scores allows researchers to evaluate ASR systems using any chosen language model configuration (see Tables 1 and 2). The AraDiaWER metric consists of two components, the syntactic component, and the semantic component, which capture different aspects of the accuracy and fluency of the predicted transcript. The syntactic component captures changes in parts of speech and lemmas, which are crucial for capturing the grammatical structure of the predicted transcript. On the other hand, the semantic component aims to capture variances in meaning and context, providing a more comprehensive and interpretable evaluation of the DA ASR system. Additionally, the use of embeddings from each LM is essential for extracting an explainable correlation between errors made by the ASR and AraDiaWER's two scores (semantic and syntactic). The transparent and interpretable nature of the AraDiaWER metric facilitates a comprehensive evaluation of the performance of DA ASR systems by accounting for the linguistic, semantic, and fluency features of dialectical Arabic speech, which are not fully captured by the traditional WER metric.

2.2.1 Syntactic Component

The syntactic component of the AraDiaWER assigns morphological and lexical tags to the reference and predicted transcripts. This has been achieved by utilizing a BERT-based disambiguation model (Inoue et al., 2021) out of the box, which uses a pre-trained CAMeLBERT-Mix language model to classify the morphological and lexical features of an input sequence. Firstly, we use CAMeLBERT-Mix LM to determine the syntactic tag. Secondly, we use a unigram-based morphosyntactic analyzer (Inoue et al., 2022)) to refine the unfactored parent tag (e.g., POS) to an individual subtag (e.g., noun).

For the purpose of our study, the output of the syntactic model was limited to the following tags: parts-of-speech (POS) tags, lemmas (lex), and five clitic features: article proclitic (prc0), preposition proclitic (prc1), conjunction proclitic (prc2), question proclitic (prc3), and pronominal enclitic (enc0). A fuzzy matching algorithm runs on the set of tags assigned for each word and calculates the syntactic score. Tables 1 and 2 show how different syntactic tag configurations affect the final weight W_{err}.

The syntactic score in Eq. 3 aims to capture the syntactic variances in the reference and predicted transcripts. It is calculated using the Levenshtein distance (LD) (Eq. 1) between the syntactic characteristics (list of POS, lexicons, and clitics) of the reference (L_{ref}) and prediction (L_{hyp}). Using the LD, the fuzzy ratio (FR) Eq. (2) is calculated for each pair of words, and the total ratio for the entire sequence is calculated by dividing the sum of the fuzzy ratios by the total number of words (N). This scoring process is repeated for each syntactic tag and the total syntactic score is the sum of the fuzzy ratios of all unfactored tags (POS, lexicons, and clitics) over the total number of sequences, a value bound between 0 and 1. The formulas are as follows.

$$\text{LD}\,(str1, str2) = \text{LevDist}\,(str1, str2) \tag{1}$$

$$\text{FR}\,(str1, str2) = \frac{(\text{len}(str1) + \text{len}(str2) - \text{LD})}{(\text{len}(str1) + \text{len}(str2))} \tag{2}$$

$$\text{ScoreSyn}\,(L_{\text{ref}}, L_{\text{hyp}}) = \frac{\sum_i^N (\text{FR}_i\,(L_{\text{ref,i}}, L_{\text{hyp,i}}))}{N} \tag{3}$$

2.2.2 Semantic Component

The semantic score of AraDiaWER aims to capture contextual differences between the reference and predicted transcripts by using the pre-trained MiniLM sentence transformer (Wang et al., 2020) out of the box. This language model is designed to perform various NLP tasks, such as feature extraction, question answering, natural language generation, question generation, abstractive summarization, and more. Our semantic scoring component uses the 6-layer all-MiniLM-L6-v2 variant to vectorize the input sequences and perform cosine similarity calculations on the resulting high-dimensional vectors.

Our semantic component focuses specifically on the contextual differences between the reference and predicted transcripts, which are not captured by syntactic information alone. By encoding the prediction and reference transcript pairs (e_{pre},e_{ref}), using the MiniLM language model, the cosine similarity is calculated to obtain the semantic score, as shown in Eq. 4. This allows the capture of the contextual differences between the reference and predicted transcripts, which are indicative of the semantic differences.

$$\text{ScoreSem}\,(e_{\text{ref}}, e_{\text{hyp}}) = \frac{(e_{\text{ref}})^T \cdot e_{\text{hyp}}}{\|e_{\text{ref}}\| \cdot \|e_{\text{hyp}}\|} \tag{4}$$

2.2.3 Error Weight & AraDiaWER

In our AraDiaWER metric, we introduced an error weight (W_{err}) to determine the influence of semantic and syntactic changes that occur in the language on the estimation of the errors made by ASR systems. Our error weight is based on the theory of weighted sums and weighted averages. In statistics, it is important to account for biases in the data by looking at possible variances within the sample. For example, using variance σ_i^2, we can compose a weight $\frac{1}{\sigma_i^2}$ that can be used to calculate the weighted average of all measurements to obtain an estimate of a signal. Using the weighted sum approach, we take the syntactic and semantic variances of a sample and build a weight function using the following formula:

$$W_{\text{err}} = \frac{1}{\text{ScoreSem} + \text{ScoreSyn}} \tag{5}$$

By incorporating our error weight into the AraDiaWER metric, we obtain a more comprehensive and interpretable evaluation of DA ASR systems, which takes into account syntactic and semantic variances. The estimated errors are calculated using the new AraDiaWER function, which is a weighted sum of the errors based on their corresponding error weight. WER is computed by summing up all substitutions, insertions, and deletions and dividing them by the total number of words in the reference transcript. AraDiaWER computes WER in terms of a weighted sum of errors, as shown in Eq. 7

WER is the sum of all substitutions, insertions, and deletions (SUB, INS, and DEL) on the total number of words in the reference (N_{ref}), which includes correct words (HIT). The formulas are as follows.

$$\text{WER} = \frac{\text{SUB} + \text{INS} + \text{DEL}}{\text{SUB} + \text{DEL} + \text{HIT}} \tag{6}$$

$$\text{AraDiaWER} = \frac{WER}{ScoreSem + ScoreSyn} \tag{7}$$

The relationship between WER and AraDiaWER in terms of ranking or score correlation can be interpreted as follows: AraDiaWER refines the standard WER by incorporating the error weight, which considers both semantic and syntactic variances. As a result, the AraDiaWER values will generally be correlated with WER but provide a more nuanced ranking of ASR systems, as it accounts for these variances in the Egyptian Arabic dialects.

In order to ensure the interpretability and practical relevance of the AraDiaWER metric, it is necessary to impose a constraint on the syntactic and semantic scores. Specifically, both ScoreSem and ScoreSyn must exceed a threshold of 0.5. This requirement guarantees that the error weight remains within a reasonable range, avoiding excessively large or small values that could undermine the metric's interpretability. By stipulating that ScoreSem and ScoreSyn surpass 0.5, we preserve a balanced representation of the semantic and syntactic variances within the AraDiaWER metric, thereby facilitating more accurate and reliable evaluations of DA ASR systems.

The use of the error weight in our AraDiaWER metric is crucial in assessing the performance of DA ASR systems. The weight determines the importance of semantic and syntactic variances, and it ensures that the evaluation is not biased toward a particular component. This approach allows a better understanding of the performance of ASR systems in dialectical Arabic speech and provides more accurate and reliable evaluations.

2.3 Quantitative Analysis of Syntactic and Semantic Errors

The main objective of AraDiaWER is to explain the performance of ASR systems in terms of syntactic and semantic errors. We calculate the Pearson correlation between the WER errors (SUB, INS, DEL) made by the ASR system and the semantic and syntactic scores. The correlation analysis helps to understand which type of errors the ASR system is making and how those errors are reflected in the semantic and syntactic scores. We also utilized p-values to determine the statistical significance of the correlations. By analyzing the correlation and p-values, we can determine the strengths and weaknesses of the ASR system and identify areas for improvement. This information can be used to optimize the ASR system and improve its overall performance. Additionally, the use of AraDiaWER allows for a more interpretable and transparent assessment of the ASR system's performance, making it easier to communicate the results to stakeholders and end-users. The AraDiaWER metric provides a more comprehensive and interpretable assessment of ASR system performance in order to make recommendations based on the traceable assessment. For instance, we can identify the areas where the ASR system is underperforming and recommend improvements to the language models or training data.

2.4 Qualitative Analysis using UMAP & Language Models

To analyze the fluency of the predicted transcript, we measure perplexity and combine it with quantitative results to provide a clear assessment of ASR performance. We measure the perplexity score using a dedicated language model. In our implementation, we use GPT-2 base model (Radford et al., 2019) to measure perplexity, and the inverse of perplexity is reported as fluency. Another key component in the quality analysis is the comparison of the reference and prediction embeddings. Our objective is to visualize the semantic embeddings of references and predictions in a low-dimensional space using UMAP to determine overlaps between reference and prediction samples; more dispersed overlaps can indicate better performance.

The UMAP projections for the Whisper ASR model, as shown in Figure 3, provide a way to visualize the quality of the ASR output in a 2D space. By looking at the 2-component UMAP projections for references and hypotheses in different datasets, we can assess the ability of the ASR system to generalize and capture the unique linguistic features of the target dialect. For instance, the UMAP projection for the MGB3 test set, as shown in Figure 3b, shows a low-quality projection, indicating a poor performance of the Whisper model on this dataset. Conversely, the UMAP projection for the FLEURS test set, as shown in Figure 3d, shows an excellent projection, indicating that the Whisper model was able to capture the unique features of this dataset well. The UMAP projections provide an additional tool for evaluating the performance of ASR models, beyond just quantitative metrics. It enables a visual representation of the quality of the ASR output that can aid in identifying areas for improvement and optimizing ASR systems.

The semantic and syntactic scores are used in conjunction with other evaluation metrics, such as the ASR model fluency and the quality of UMAP projections, to provide a more comprehensive and interpretable assessment of the performance of DA ASR systems. Figure 4 shows the comparison between the Whisper scores and the transcript fluency and overall quality extracted from UMAP projections. The figure highlights the negative correlation between the semantic scores and transcript fluency,

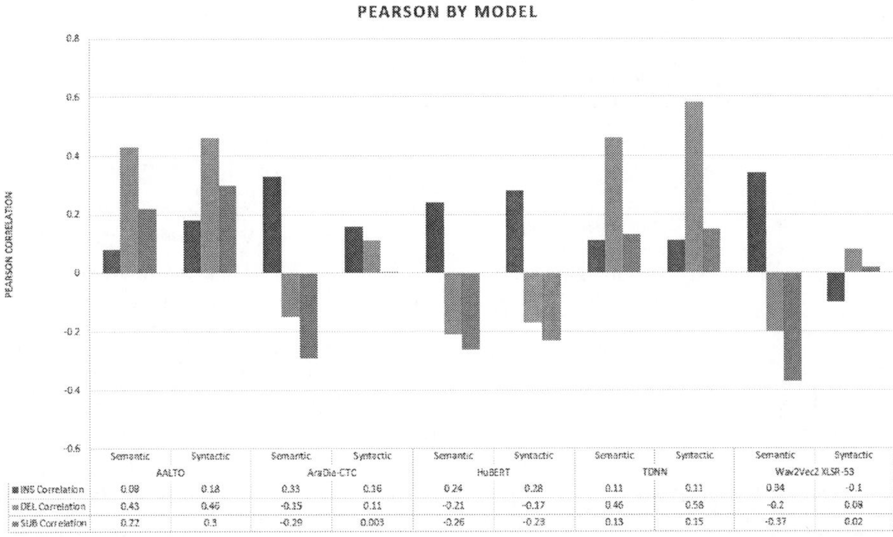

Figure 2: A grouped bar chart showing the semantic and syntactic correlations of different ASR models with AraDiaWER. The bars show the Pearson correlation coefficients of the WER SUB, DEL, and INS. The results indicate that the correlations between semantic errors and WER are generally negative, while the correlations between syntactic errors and WER are generally positive. AALTO and TDNN show strong correlations with both semantic and syntactic errors, while Wav2Vec2 XLSR-53 and HuBERT show negative correlations with semantic errors and weaker positive correlations with syntactic errors. AraDia-CTC, on the other hand, shows strong negative correlations with semantic errors and positive correlations with syntactic errors. In the context of the paper, positive correlation means that when the WER errors increase, the corresponding semantic or syntactic errors also increase, while negative correlation means that when the WER errors decrease, the corresponding semantic or syntactic errors decrease.

	Avg	Semantic Correlation with WER			Syntactic Correlation with WER		
Model	Sem/Syn Error	SUB Pearson / pVal	DEL Pearson / pVal	INS Pearson / pVal	SUB Pearson / pVal	DEL Pearson / pVal	INS Pearson / pVal
AALTO	0.07 / 0.16	0.22 / 1.08E-11	0.43 / 2.21E-47	0.08 / 1.41E-02	0.30 / 2.22E-21	0.46 / 1.86E-54	0.18/ 5.43E-09
TDNN	0.16 / 0.33	0.13 / 8.76E-09	0.46 / 4.28E-109	0.11 / 3.86E-07	0.15 / 5.83E-12	0.58 / 7.42E-184	0.11 / 7.97E-07
Wav2Vec2 XLSR-53	0.19 / 0.47	-0.37 / 2.97E-11	-0.20 / 6.20E-04	0.34 / 1.96E-09	0.02 / 7.61E-01	0.08 / 1.66E-01	-0.10 / 8.08E-02
HuBERT	0.15 / 0.30	-0.26 / 4.47E-06	-0.21 / 2.34E-04	0.24 / 2.18E-05	-0.23 / 8.56E-05	-0.17 / 3.67E-03	0.28 / 9.42E-07
AraDia-CTC	0.15 / 0.33	-0.29 / 5.83E-07	-0.15 / 1.19E-02	0.33 / 5.17E-09	0.003 / 9.51E-01	0.11 / 5.82E-02	0.16 / 4.75E-03

Table 3: AraDiaWER Correlations with Semantic and Syntactic Errors

System	Dataset	WER	AraDia WER	RMSE
AALTO	MGB3(A)	0.400	0.268	0.11
TDNN	MGB3(D)	0.710	0.604	**0.09**
Wav2Vec2 XLSR-53	FLEURS	0.600	0.470	0.12
HuBERT	FLEURS	0.480	0.330	0.14
AraDia-CTC	FLEURS	0.540	0.400	0.13
Whisper	FLEURS	**0.210**	**0.120**	0.10

Table 4: Results on the MGB-3 and FLEURS datasets extracted from the study. (D) is the development set and (A) is the adaptation set.

System	WER	AraDia WER	RMSE
AALTO	**0.400**	**0.268**	0.11
TDNN	0.710	0.604	**0.09**
Wav2Vec2 XLSR-53	0.753	0.660	**0.09**
HuBERT	0.733	0.580	0.18
AraDia-CTC	0.695	0.575	0.12
Whisper	0.565	0.446	0.15

Table 5: Average results across all tests. AALTO captures the Egyptian dialect well, while Whisper is capable of generalizing to any dataset.

indicating that the higher the semantic score, the lower the fluency of the transcript. On the other hand, the transcript quality is impacted the most when the ASR model commits more syntactic errors. This suggests that the syntactic score is more sensitive to the variations in the ASR output across different dialects, making it a useful tool for identifying areas for improvement in DA ASR systems.

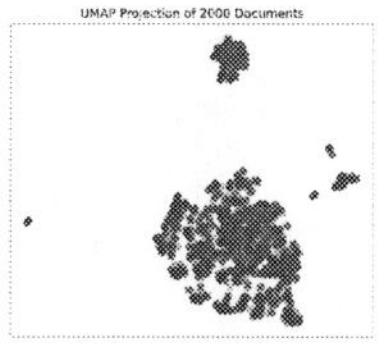

(a) 2-component UMAP for references and hypotheses in CommonVoice 6.1 (Good)

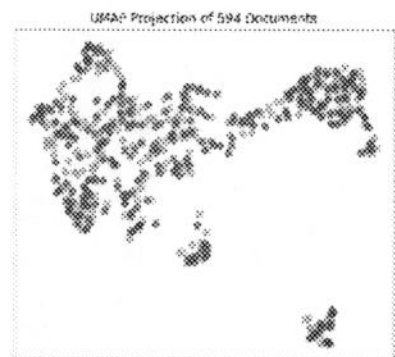

(b) 2-component UMAP for references and hypotheses in MGB3 test set (Poor)

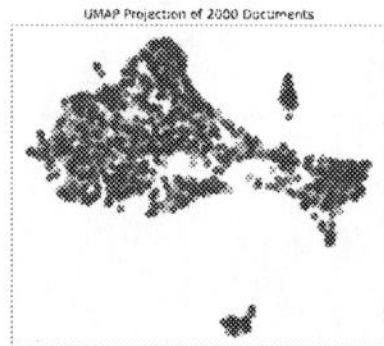

(c) 2-component UMAP for references and hypotheses in MGB2 train set (Good)

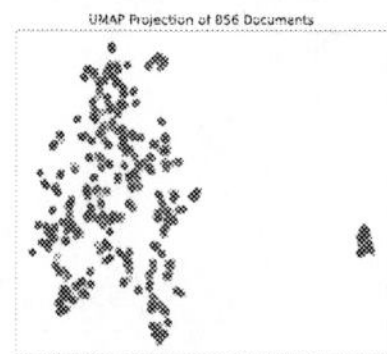

(d) 2-component UMAP for references and hypotheses in FLEURS test set (Excellent)

Figure 3: UMAP projections for Whisper ASR model in different datasets. The scatter plots show 2-component UMAP projections of references and hypotheses for (a) CommonVoice 6.1, (b) MGB3 test set, (c) MGB2 train set, and (d) FLEURS test set. The UMAP projections help assess the quality of the ASR output and the similarity between reference and hypotheses.

The use of multiple evaluation metrics, including the semantic and syntactic scores, transcript fluency, and UMAP projections, enables us to obtain a more complete picture of the performance of DA ASR systems and make more informed recommendations for improving their performance.

3 Results and Analysis

Table 3 illustrates the results of our experiments, which aim to evaluate the AraDiaWER metric's effectiveness in assessing ASR systems in dialectal Arabic. The evaluated models include AALTO, TDNN, Wav2Vec2 XLSR-53, HuBERT, and AraDia-CTC. The average semantic and syntactic errors are presented in the table. We observe that the TDNN model has the highest average semantic and syntactic errors, followed by Wav2Vec2 XLSR-53, AraDia-CTC, AALTO, and HuBERT. The results show that the AraDiaWER metric is effective in capturing the syntactic and semantic errors of ASR systems and that different LM models have varying degrees of performance in capturing these errors. Our approach relies on the semantic and syntactic components of AraDiaWER. The semantic component measures the variances in meaning and context between the reference and predicted transcripts, while the syntactic component captures the syntactic variations in dialectal utterances. The results show that the semantic correlation with WER is generally negative, while the syntactic correlation with WER is positive. The AALTO and TDNN models have high syntactic correlations with WER, indicating that these models have significant syntactic errors. On the other hand, Wav2Vec2 XLSR-53, HuBERT, and AraDia-CTC have low syntactic correlations with WER, indicating that these models have low syntactic errors. Furthermore, the AraDia-CTC model has the highest semantic correlation with WER, indicating that it has the highest semantic errors among the models evaluated. Conversely, the TDNN model has the lowest semantic correlation with WER, indicating that it has the lowest semantic errors among the models. The experimental results show that the p-values of the correlations are all statistically significant ($p < 0.05$) which provides insight into the underlying factors that contribute to the ASR system's performance.

Tables 4 and 5 summarize the results for each system. The averaged results of AALTO showed that the best performance is observed when a system is trained and tested in a fully supervised approach on the same distribution and language. The results of TDNN show that even legacy systems can perform well when it comes to capturing syntactic and semantic patterns. This is further proven in the ablation studies for AALTO and TDNN, where the number of syntactic tags captured is negatively correlated with the penalty-reducing error weight W_{err} (see Tables 1 and 2). Linking this to the correlation analysis in AALTO, it is possible to deduce that capturing additional syntactic tags can lead to improved syntactic scores and better overall capture of dialectical variations in utterances, decreasing the error weight and AraDiaWER value. Higher semantic scores indicate a better contextual understanding of the utterance, allowing for more accurate prediction of words that are similar and reducing the RMSE between WER and AraDiaWER. In addition, less complex utterances observe higher syntactic and semantic scores. Lastly, certain outliers in the dataset still achieve high semantic and syntactic scores but fail at fluency; this shows the metric's ability to pinpoint low-quality utterances that are not intelligible. The inclusion of RMSE in the calculation of the results serves as a means of

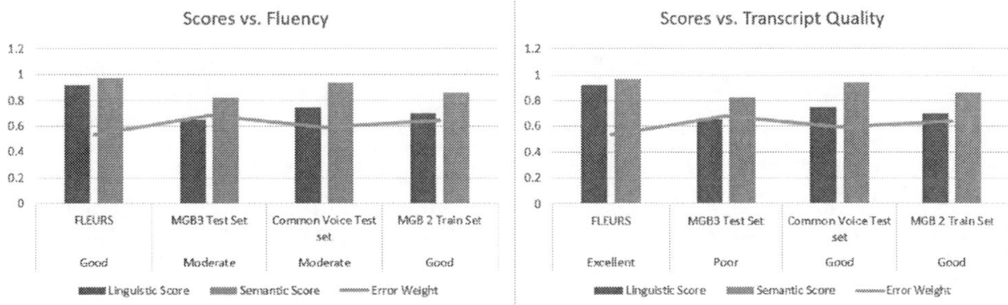

Figure 4: Comparison of Whisper ASR scores with transcript fluency and overall quality extracted from UMAP projections. The labels 'Excellent', 'Good', 'Moderate', and 'Poor' indicate the visual quality of the UMAP projections and the range of Perplexity values for the ASR model output. The scatter plots show the correlation between the semantic, syntactic, and AraDiaWER scores with the transcript fluency and overall quality. The results indicate that AraDiaWER is positively correlated with the overall quality of the ASR output, while the semantic and syntactic scores show a stronger correlation with transcript fluency. These findings highlight the usefulness of AraDiaWER as a more comprehensive and interpretable metric for evaluating DA ASR systems.

quantifying the differences between WER and AraDiaWER. By measuring the RMSE, we can assess the degree of agreement between the two metrics and determine the extent to which AraDiaWER captures variations in dialectal Arabic speech that are not fully represented by the traditional WER. This additional analysis provides further insight into the strengths and limitations of AraDiaWER, enabling researchers and practitioners to better understand the implications of adopting this new metric in the context of DA ASR systems evaluation.

The experimental study reveals that the use of AraDiaWER brings an average improvement of 18.65% in error rate compared to WER. This improvement does not necessarily suggest that our metric is a direct replacement for WER or that it outperforms it in all aspects. Rather, our approach offers a transparent and traceable method that utilizes language models to evaluate DA ASR systems in a more comprehensive and interpretable manner.

4 Conclusion

The focus of this paper is to propose an explainable evaluation metric, AraDiaWER, that complements WER and is designed to assess the performance of Automatic Speech Recognition (ASR) systems for dialectal Arabic speech. This metric combines three different scoring systems, namely syntactic, semantic, and fluency, by utilizing state-of-the-art models. The main objective of AraDiaWER is to provide a more detailed and inclusive assessment of the performance of ASR systems in the context of dialectal Arabic speech, which is a significant improvement compared to the conventional word error rate (WER) metric alone.

This work can be considered a resource tool to capture the dialectal variations in speech, where the addition of syntactic features, such as parts of speech tags and lemmas, is helpful for improving the overall performance of the metric. Moreover, the incorporation of semantic features allows the ASR to be evaluated based on meaning, thus ensuring a more holistic assessment of the ASR system. Therefore, we do not seek to undermine the importance of WER but to offer a complementary tool that enables a more extensible evaluation of DA ASR systems

The AraDiaWER framework relies on language models (LMs) to extract both syntactic and semantic features from the text. While LMs are primarily trained for syntactic features, they also contain information about semantic features. The syntactic component assigns morphological and lexical tags to the text using the embeddings of CAMeLBERT-Mix LM. The semantic component uses the embeddings of MiniLM and cosine similarity to calculate the semantic similarity between the reference and predicted transcripts. The embeddings of each LM are used to extract explainable correlations between errors made by the ASR and AraDiaWER's two scores (semantic, and syntactic). This allows us to capture both semantic and syntactic features and make more comprehensive and interpretable assessments of the ASR systems. Additionally, the proposed evaluation framework uses a UMAP analysis to evaluate the semantic patterns in a low-dimensional space and the GPT-2 generated perplexity score to determine the fluency of an utterance.

In conclusion, while there is still room for improvement, our proposed AraDiaWER metric represents a step forward in the comprehensive evaluation of ASR systems, especially in the context of dialectal variations. In future work, we plan to further improve the metric by incorporating multilingual language models to capture additional morphological and orthographic patterns in the transcripts, target a wider range of diverse datasets, and use modern LMs like GPT-4, LaMDA, and LLaMA to interpret perplexity and AraDiaWER results even further for a more detailed analogy.

Limitations

One of the limitations is the reliance on the available language models for calculating the semantic and syntactic scores. The quality of these scores may depend on the training data and domain specificity, which may have an impact on the generalizability of our findings. Additionally, the scope of our experiments is limited to one set of Arabic dialects, namely Egyptian, which may not be representative of all dialectical variations in the language. Further work is needed to evaluate the effectiveness of the AraDiaWER metric on a wider range of dialects and to improve the quality of the language models used in our study.

Ethics Statement

In compliance with the ACL Ethics Policy, we acknowledge the potential ethical considerations associated with this research on automatic speech recognition for dialectical Arabic. The proposed AraDiaWER metric is intended to provide a more comprehensive and explainable evaluation of DA ASR systems that can better account for dialectical variations. However, we acknowledge the potential impact of any inaccuracies in the system, particularly regarding sociocultural implications. As such, we urge caution in the use and application of this metric and encourage future research to further explore the impact of such technology on diverse groups and communities. We are committed to ethical research practices and will prioritize transparency and accountability in all future studies.

References

Ahmed Ali, Salam Khalifa, and Nizar Habash. 2019. Towards variability resistant dialectal speech evaluation: 20th Annual Conference of the International Speech Communication Association: Crossroads of Speech and Language, INTERSPEECH 2019. *Proceedings of the Annual Conference of the International Speech Communication Association, INTERSPEECH*, 2019-September:336–340.

Ahmed Ali, Walid Magdy, and Steve Renals. 2015. Multi-Reference Evaluation for Dialectal Speech Recognition System: A Study for Egyptian ASR. In *Proceedings of the Second Workshop on Arabic Natural Language Processing*, pages 118–126, Beijing, China. Association for Computational Linguistics.

Ahmed Ali, Preslav Nakov, Peter Bell, and Steve Renals. 2017. WERd: Using Social Text Spelling Variants for Evaluating Dialectal Speech Recognition. Technical Report arXiv:1709.07484, arXiv. ArXiv:1709.07484 [cs] type: article.

Ahmed Ali and Steve Renals. 2020. Word Error Rate Estimation Without ASR Output: e-WER2. Technical Report arXiv:2008.03403, arXiv. ArXiv:2008.03403 [cs, eess] type: article.

Ahmed Ali, Yifan Zhang, Patrick Cardinal, Najim Dahak, Stephan Vogel, and James Glass. 2014. A complete KALDI recipe for building Arabic speech recognition systems. In *2014 IEEE Spoken Language Technology Workshop (SLT)*, pages 525–529.

Ahmed M. Ali and S. Renals. 2018. Word Error Rate Estimation for Speech Recognition: e-WER. In *ACL*.

Alexei Baevski, Henry Zhou, Abdelrahman Mohamed, and Michael Auli. 2020. wav2vec 2.0: A Framework for Self-Supervised Learning of Speech Representations. *arXiv:2006.11477 [cs, eess]*. ArXiv: 2006.11477.

Naman Goyal, Cynthia Gao, Vishrav Chaudhary, Peng-Jen Chen, Guillaume Wenzek, Da Ju, Sanjana Krishnan, Marc'Aurelio Ranzato, Francisco Guzman, and Angela Fan. 2021. The FLORES-101 Evaluation Benchmark for Low-Resource and Multilingual Machine Translation. ArXiv:2106.03193 [cs].

Wei-Ning Hsu, Benjamin Bolte, Yao-Hung Hubert Tsai, Kushal Lakhotia, Ruslan Salakhutdinov, and Abdelrahman Mohamed. 2021. HuBERT: Self-Supervised Speech Representation Learning by Masked Prediction of Hidden Units. *arXiv:2106.07447 [cs, eess]*. ArXiv: 2106.07447.

Go Inoue, Bashar Alhafni, Nurpeiis Baimukan, Houda Bouamor, and Nizar Habash. 2021. The Interplay of Variant, Size, and Task Type in Arabic Pre-trained Language Models. In *Proceedings of the Sixth Arabic Natural Language Processing Workshop*, pages 92–104, Kyiv, Ukraine (Virtual). Association for Computational Linguistics.

Go Inoue, Salam Khalifa, and Nizar Habash. 2022. Morphosyntactic Tagging with Pre-trained Language Models for Arabic and its Dialects. ArXiv:2110.06852 [cs].

Suyoun Kim, Abhinav Arora, Duc Le, Ching-Feng Yeh, Christian Fuegen, Ozlem Kalinli, and Michael L. Seltzer. 2021. Semantic Distance: A New Metric for ASR Performance Analysis Towards Spoken Language Understanding. ArXiv:2104.02138 [cs].

Kathrein Abu Kwaik, Motaz Saad, Stergios Chatzikyriakidis, and Simon Dobnika. 2018. A Lexical Distance Study of Arabic Dialects. *Procedia Computer Science*, 142:2–13.

Vimal Manohar, Daniel Povey, and Sanjeev Khudanpur. 2017. JHU Kaldi system for Arabic MGB-3 ASR challenge using diarization, audio-transcript alignment and transfer learning. In *2017 IEEE Automatic Speech Recognition and Understanding Workshop (ASRU)*, pages 346–352.

Maryam Najafian, Wei-Ning Hsu, Ahmed Ali, and James Glass. 2017. Automatic speech recognition of Arabic multi-genre broadcast media. In *2017 IEEE Automatic Speech Recognition and Understanding Workshop (ASRU)*, pages 353–359.

Alec Radford, John Kim, and Xu. 2022. Robust Speech Recognition via Large-Scale Weak Supervision.

Alec Radford, Jeff Wu, Rewon Child, David Luan, Dario Amodei, and Ilya Sutskever. 2019. Language models are unsupervised multitask learners.

Peter Smit, Siva Reddy Gangireddy, Seppo Enarvi, Sami Virpioja, and Mikko Kurimo. 2017. Aalto system for the 2017 Arabic multi-genre broadcast challenge. In *2017 IEEE Automatic Speech Recognition and Understanding Workshop (ASRU)*, pages 338–345.

Karel Vesely, Murali Karthick Baskar, Mireia Diez, and Karel Benes. 2017. MGB-3 but system: Low-resource ASR on Egyptian YouTube data. pages 368–373.

Wenhui Wang, Furu Wei, Li Dong, Hangbo Bao, Nan Yang, and Ming Zhou. 2020. MiniLM: Deep Self-Attention Distillation for Task-Agnostic Compression of Pre-Trained Transformers. ArXiv:2002.10957 [cs].

A Quest for Paradigm Coverage: The Story of Nen

Saliha Muradoğlu♣♠ Hanna Suominen♣◇ Nicholas Evans♣♠
♣The Australian National University (ANU) ◇University of Turku
♠ARC Centre of Excellence for the Dynamics of Language (CoEDL)
Firstname.Lastname@anu.edu.au

Abstract

Language documentation aims to collect a representative corpus of the language. Nevertheless, the question of how to quantify the comprehensive of the collection persists. We propose leveraging computational modelling to provide a supplementary metric to address this question in a low-resource language setting. We apply our proposed methods to the Papuan language Nen. Nen is actively in the process of being described and documented. Given the enormity of the task of language documentation, we focus on one subdomain, namely Nen verbal morphology. This study examines four verb types: copula, positional, middle, and transitive. We propose model-based paradigm generation for each verb type as a new way to measure completeness, where accuracy is analogous to the coverage of the paradigm. We contrast the paradigm attestation within the corpus (constructed from fieldwork data) and the accuracy of the paradigm generated by Transformer models trained for inflection. This analysis is extended by extrapolating from the learning curve established to provide predictions for the quantity of data required to generate a complete paradigm correctly. We also explore the correlation between high-frequency morphosyntactic features and model accuracy. We see a positive correlation between high-frequency feature combinations and model accuracy, but this is only sometimes the case. We also see high accuracy for low-frequency morphosyntactic features. Our results show that model coverage is significantly higher for the middle and transitive verbs but not the positional verb. This is an interesting finding, as the positional verb paradigm is the smallest of the four.

1 Introduction

A key question in studying language is: when do we have enough data to fully understand the system? This is especially important in language documentation. As Himmelmann (1998) states, *'the aim of language documentation is to provide a comprehensive record of the linguistic practices characteristic of a given speech community.'*. Bird (2015) extends this by asking, *'If a comprehensive record is unattainable in principle, is there a consensus on what an adequate record looks like. How would you quantify it?'*.

Honouring their formulation, Baird et al. (2022) label this the 'Himmelman-Bird' problem.[1] In their paper, the authors strive to explore this Himmelman-Bird problem for the inventory of phonemes, which are the subdomain of language with the smallest and hence most frequently-occurring units. They set the bar even lower by simply requiring that at least one allophone of each phoneme occur. They then examine how much text it might take to capture a language's entire phoneme inventory, drawing on a sample of 137 distinct languages, some with additional dialectal or register variety taking the total to 158 speech varieties. Full 'coverage' is achieved, for a given domain of language (say, its phoneme inventory) and a given corpus, it there is at least one incidence of each relevant unit (in this case, each phoneme) in that corpus.

Here we strive to follow a similar route for morphemes and their respective allomorphs, while still posing the problem in its simplest and hence most easily-satisfied form: we look just at verbs, and we restrict ourselves to one representative lexeme (the commonest) in each of the four main morphological classes – see below.

The goal of collecting a representative sample has permeated many fields, from biology to sociology. Researchers have explored the idea of having a gold standard process for collecting all required components to describe a system. For example, if we wanted to gather all the phonemes for English, the 'Rainbow Passage' by Fairbanks (1960) may be chosen. The first four lines of the passage cap-

[1] This is akin to the problem of corpus representativity.

Proceedings of the Second Workshop on NLP Applications to Field Linguistics, pages 74–85
May 6, 2023 ©2023 Association for Computational Linguistics

ture all phonemes for English. In morphology, we can discuss the idea of collecting all principal parts (Finkel and Stump, 2007) to construct the entire paradigm.

This idea presents as a great solution to the difficulty faced by low-resource languages and, more specifically, language documentation. However, one caveat is the system knowledge required for designing such a task. For example, how might a linguist know all the phonemes before beginning their in-field analysis and recordings? Accordingly, we make the distinction between heuristic and attestation coverage.

The first refers to the discovery stage of a language, leading to a sketching of the dimensions of its design space - the logical space of all its possibilities in a particular domain, such as verbal inflections – through discovering the dimensions where it encodes contrasts (say 'dual number', 'future imperative', 'imperfect aspect'), and mapping out the ways these interact (say 'future imperfective dual imperative', as in Nen *nandowabe* 'you two should be talking later on!' (Evans, 2019). The latter describes the scenario where a description exists, and the aim is to collect examples of language within the denoted design space.

The concept of a 'whole language' is so vast and heterogenous that it is not operationally useful for many linguistic or practical purposes. To explore this question, we consider a particular component of language, inflectional morphology on the verb. We base our study on modelling morphological inflection in the Nen language and examine the attestation coverage observed in the transcribed natural spoken corpus and inflection models built on the same data.

In this paper, we address the following questions: (1) How can we test the degree to which a linguistic subsystem exhibits coverage in a given corpus (2) How does the model coverage compare with the corpus? (3) Does corpus frequency relate to model accuracy? (4) Can we use model-based learning curves to predict the data required for complete coverage?

We propose a test case for the model that asks to predict a complete paradigm, i.e. the complete multidimensional array of inflected forms – English is too morphologically impoverished to furnish a good example (the best is with the copula to be: {*am, (art), is, are; was, were; (to) be; being*}. Our results indicate that the generalisations afforded by the Transformer model yield better coverage than the natural corpus. Furthermore, we explore two separate correlations of the high dimensional axes of Nen verbs; the undergoer and agent combinations and the agent and Tense, Aspect, and Mood (TAM) combinations. While frequent features tend to be captured correctly by the model, surprisingly, so are some low-frequency forms. Finally, we use learning curves to predict the data needed for 100% coverage.

2 Related Work

To our knowledge, only two prior computational studies of Nen exist. Muradoglu et al. (2020) presents a finite-state description, while (Muradoğlu et al., 2020) explores the use of neural architecture, to model Nen verbal morphology. The latter is based on two high performing submissions in the SIGMORPHON–CoNLL 2017 Shared Task (Cotterell et al., 2017). Between the two approaches, the finite-state description achieves a higher accuracy across the corpus. However, we note that the accuracies reported are not directly comparable given the ongoing development of the corpus.

Despite the performance difference, we opt to use a neural approach to enlist the aid of its generalising ability. Moreover, the statistical nature of these models make the intersect with corpus linguistics an object of interest. Specifically, we use a Transformer (Vaswani et al., 2017) based model. Transformers have been successful in capturing complexities of phonological and morphological details (Pimentel et al., 2021; Kodner et al., 2022), often achieving state-of-the-art performance. Over the years, the inflection task has been extended to many languages, including other complex morphological systems such as Murrinh-Patha, Kunwinjku and Seneca.

3 The Nen Language

Nen is a Papuan language of the Morehead-Maro (or Yam) family (Evans, 2017). It is spoken as a native language in the village of Bimadbn in the Western Province of Papua New Guinea (Evans, 2015, 2019). Most Nen speakers are multilingual, typically speaking several of the neighbouring languages.

Verbs in Nen are notoriously complicated and are described as the most complicated word-class in Nen (Evans, 2015, 2019). They can be grouped in several ways, either as prefixing and ambifixing or by further breaking down the inflection patterns. Prefixing verbs consist of the copula (and its derivatives 'go'/'come'/'have'), 'to walk' and positional verbs. Another distinguishing feature of prefixing verbs, is the lack of infinitives. Both ambifixing and middle verbs form infinitives through suffixing *-s* to the verb stem. In this study, we have listed the prefixing verb lemmas as the verb stem. Ambifixing verbs can be separated into middle and transitive verbs. Here, we separate the verb types beyond the prefixing and ambifixing categories as the corresponding paradigms are distinct. We provide details for the verbs we track below.

3.1 Copula

The copula is a special case for our test, in that we test the generation of a partial paradigm as the model would have seen several forms of the copula. We note that this verb, together with its directional counterparts 'come' and 'go'. The come/go paradigms are built using the copula with the addition of directional prefixes, is the most frequent verb type in the corpus. The copula paradigm consists of 40 unique forms. See Evans (2014) for full paradigm.

3.2 Positional

Verbs in the positional class fall into two main types: posture and position proper (Evans, 2015). For example, *mängr* 'be lying in a jumble' and *érningr* 'be in hiding' or spatial position in relation to some frame of reference like *pingr* 'to be high (typically inanimate)'. So far, 45 verbs have been recorded. Verbs of this class have special stative suffixes *-ngr* for non-dual and *-aran* (dual). They exhibit properties of prefixing verbs: they do not have infinitives and cannot form present imperative (Evans, 2014).

3.3 Middle

Middle and transitive verbs have the same TAM paradigm. Aside from valency, the distinction between the two is that the middle verbs have a dummy prefix with no semantic meaning other than to note that they are middle verbs. This prefix does not mark an argument like other verb types. In rare cases, middle verbs use the undergoer prefix slot to index large plurals. Example verbs of this type include *owabs* 'to speak' or *angs̄* 'to return'. Both these verbs are ambifixing, but the prefixal slot is restricted to {*n-*} (α–series), {*k-*} (β–series), {*g-*} (γ–series).

3.4 Transitive

By contrast, transitive verbs utilize both prefixes and suffixes to mark person and number. Examples of this verb type include *yis* 'to plant' and *waprs* 'to do' These verbs allow for full prefixing and suffixing possibilities. The prefix set is divided through the use of the same arbitrarily labels α, β, and γ, as the middle verbs. Instead of the middle verb marker, transitive verbs allow for person/number undergoer marking. These dummy indices do not carry specific semantic values until they are unified with other TAM markings on the verb.

Evans (2016) provides the canonical paradigms for the undergoer prefixes, thematics and desinences. Suffixes are constructed by combining the corresponding thematic and the desinence. The future imperative construction is a special case, where an additional future imperative prefix is required (Evans, 2015).

3.5 Directional

Following the undergoer prefixes, a directional prefix slot is available. This can be filled with {*-n-*} 'towards', {*-ng-*} 'away' or left empty to convey a directionally neutral semantic.

Consider the copula verb *m* 'to be', when marked for direction the resultant forms are as follows: *y-n-m* '(s)he coming (towards speaker)', *y-ng-m* '(s)he is going (away from speaker)'. Note the speaker centric frame of reference.

4 Data

The Nen corpus is made of 44 individual texts that were naturalistically recorded in the field. This amalgamates to approximately 8 hours of spoken text or over 30,000 words. This is filtered to over 6,000 verb instances representing 2,282 forms. Some of these forms are the same, with different feature combinations due to syncretism or polysemy. For example, the sequence *yn-* can be parsed in two ways. It can either mean the prefix *yn-* coding first person nonsingular undergoer for the α series or *y-n* the third singular undergoer with the ventive (towards) directional. Each of these instances are treated separately to expose the model to all possible meanings.

A large portion of the texts in the corpus are

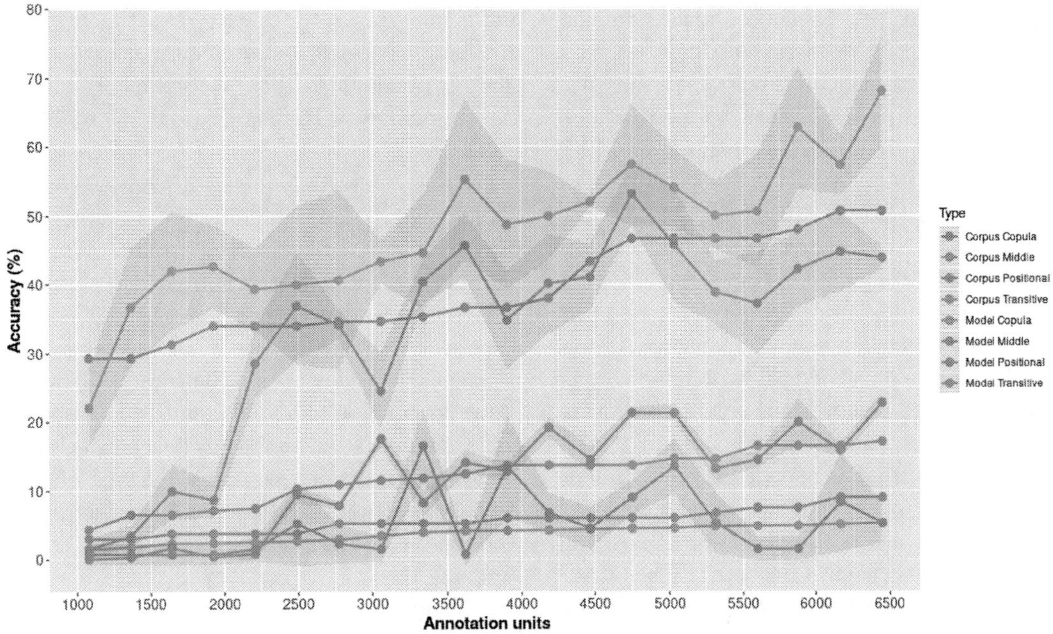

Figure 1: The coverage growth for four verb types in Nen, reported as a function of Annotation units (within corpus), where 'annotation units' are audibly-demarcated units in the flow of speech (typically by pause breaks). In our corpus, on average there is one verb per annotation unit, making annotation units a reasonable proxy of how often we would expect verbs to occur. The corpus accounts follow *akingr* 'to be standing' for the positional, *owabs* 'to speak' for the middle and *räms* 'to do/give' for the transitive. The confidence bands reported on the model results are calculated based on a 4-partition variance. The full Nen corpus currently consists of 6,446 annotation units. The starting point is 1,079 as this roughly corresponds to 382 (100 train + 282 dev) instances.

coconut interviews[2], these typically involve so-called biographical questions (parent names, place of birth etc), and questions about coconut trees that belong to the interviewee. This type of text was chosen as it can include a variety of tense - whether someone has planted or will plant a coconut tree - and is a topic that easily inspires conversation from locals. Although, these do not constitute a genre in the traditional sense, they do exhibit characteristic features, such as a high token count of the verb *yis* 'to plant' and third person non-past copula *ym*. The remaining texts range from anecdotal stories, folk tales, other narratives or procedural explanations.

5 Experiment

We contrast the corpus-based account of the Nen verbal paradigm to that modelled by a Transformer model (Wu et al., 2021). Our study is conducted in two parts: first, we follow the attestation coverage of the paradigm for one representative verb for each type in the corpus. Second, we train Transformer models to generate a complete paradigm for an unseen (barring the copula) verb for each type with incremental amounts of data. We establish a learning/coverage curve for each method (Anzanello and Fogliatto, 2011; Viering and Loog, 2022). We use the term coverage here to mean the percentage of cells observed in the corpus or correctly predicted by the models out of the entire language design space.

5.1 Corpus-based Account

Here we present a corpus account of paradigm coverage. For each of our four verb types, we follow the trajectory of the lexeme.[3] As it happens the top three verbs, by frequency, are the copula (most frequent at 80.46 IPT (Items per thousand)[4], the middle verb *owabs* 'to speak' (Second most frequent lexeme in the corpus, 6.83 IPT) and the transitive

[2]See Evans (2020) for more details.

[3]Where a lexeme is a'dictionary word', i.e. the citation form of a word used in a dictionary, and uniting all its inflected forms. Thus the lexeme *run* unites the inflected forms *run, runs, ran* and *running*. In Nen the number of inflected forms per lexeme is much larger, as we shall see below.

[4]The more common metric is IPM (items per million) but given that the size of the Nen corpus is in order of thousands, we report these figures in IPT.

verb *räms*'to do/give' (Third most frequent lexeme in corpus, 6.46 IPT). We then have to descend some way down the frequency list before reaching our highest-frequency positional verb, namely *akingr* 'to be standing' (16th most frequent lexeme, 1.83 IPT).

For our four verbs, we then collate all distinct forms of the verb in question, tracking for where in the corpus it is encountered. For example, for the verb *akingr*, the first form *yakingr* is encountered at the 223rd annotation unit, the second *ynakiaran* at 242nd and so on. The texts within the corpus are concatenated, and the same order of the text is preserved for each analysis.

The copula verb *m* is included in both training and test since it makes up for a large portion of the existing corpus and occupies the top 5 most frequent forms. It is the most frequent lexeme (80.46 IPT). This scenario can be seen as a more straightforward case, as 62.5% of the copula paradigm (without the directional prefix) is attested in the complete 2,000 instance training data. So the model needs to reproduce these forms with the directional prefixes. The remaining three verb types are not encountered in training time, barring the stem.

5.2 Model-based Account

We train models like an 'inflection' task in the SIGMORPHON shared tasks (Kodner et al., 2022), with tags identifying morpho-syntactic categories. The system is asked to produce the inflected form given the lemma and morpho-syntactic tags. For example, ⟨`owabs, V;IPFV.NPHD;1SGA;M;`α`, nowabtan`⟩ or the English equivalent ⟨`talk, V;V.PTCP;PRS`[5]`, talking`⟩.

We additionally account for the copy bias reported in (Liu and Hulden, 2022) by including the three[6] (see Section 5.2.2 for details) lemmas considered during test time in the training set.

Each model is trained using a character-level Transformer (Wu et al., 2021). This model has been used as the neural baseline for the SIGMORPHON shared task on morphological inflection[7].

We train models based on a Zipfian sampling strategy, as corpora obey Zipf's law at all sample sizes (Baayen, 2001; Blevins et al., 2017). The dev set is determined as the least frequent 282 forms and is kept the same for every experiment. The distribution is calculated from the existing corpus study (Muradoğlu, 2017). We train at 100 training sample intervals, ranging from 100 to 2,000 instances.

Prior work has explored the difference between random and Zipfian sampling. For example, Muradoğlu et al. (2020) examined the difference and reported that random selection yielded better results (or a faster coverage rate). However, given our research question, what random sampling means for language documentation is unclear. With many of the corpora built by field linguists built upon a combination of standard field method practices and anthropological story gathering, the type of data collected is hardly random. As such, the model results presented in this paper are based on Zipfian sampling.

5.2.1 Design of Test

We propose a modified test case to measure paradigm coverage of the model. A lexeme is chosen for each verb type and tested for each cell or unique morphosyntactic description (MSD).

The choice of lexeme is motivated by how regular the inflection of its particular phonotactics are. With the purpose of testing generalisability, it follows that our case study verbs are regular. Although we note that limitations of this approach, namely the variation of morphs across certain phonological properties of the stem (e.g., vowel harmony).

Given resource and access limitations we have utilised the finite-state grammar for Nen (Muradoglu et al., 2020) to generate full paradigms for the positional and transitive verbs, these paradigms are later examined by a language expert. The middle verb test is based on a full paradigm that was previously verified with Nen speakers. The full copula paradigm and its directional variants are sourced from the forthcoming grammar of Nen.

In a sense our suggested test for coverage is similar to the wug test in the SIGMORPHON shared tasks (Kodner et al., 2022), but rather than general production processes of nonce words we are interested in generating complete paradigms.

5.2.2 Meet the Verbs

***m* 'to be'** The copula paradigm consists of 40 unique forms. The come/go paradigms are built using the copula with the addition of directional prefixes.

[5]Present participle

[6]Since the model is already exposed to the copula during training time, it does not need to be included again.

[7]Model parameters follow (Wu et al., 2021).

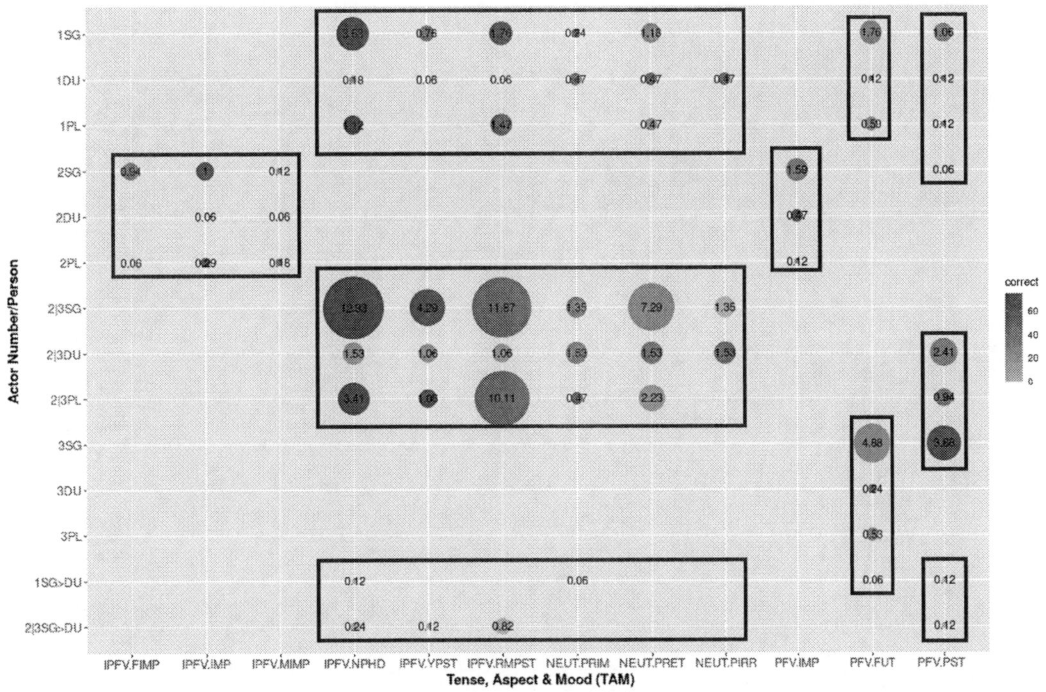

Figure 2: Bubble plot showcasing the frequency correlation between TAM and agent person number, reported numbers are percentage of corpus with the TAM/agent features. Navy lines indicate available cells described by the language design space. Note that the second and third persons are typically display syncretism except in the perfective past. See appendix A for details on TAM categories. The darker the colour (towards a blood orange) the more proficiency the model displays. Conversely the lighter the colour (orange) the more the model struggles to produce a correct form with the corresponding features.

***pingr (n-du)/piaran (du)* 'to be high/elevated'** Depending on the vowel of the stem ('i' in this case), the 2|3nsg prefix is e-, e.g., *epingr* 'you two/they two are up high'.

***armbs* 'to climb'** As with all middle verbs, *armbs* begins with a vowel. It is somewhat similar to the most common middle verb in the corpus *owabs* 'to speak', with a shared **b** before the infinitive marker *-s*. In addition to exhibiting regular inflection, the forms have been verified by native Nen speakers.

***wambaes* 'to sniff'** There are a few key points to note for this verb. When verb infinitives end with a dipthong (e.g. ae) before the final s, the dipthong is shortened in the non-dual (e.g., *wakaes* 'to look at' but *yakatan* 'I look at him/her'), but in the dual the full diphthong is present and also a dual-marking -w- which only occurs in such environments, e.g., *yawakataewn* 'I look at the two of them', *yakataewm* 'we two look at him/her'.

The most notable verb that is similar in phonological structure is *wakaes* 'to see'. The corpus contains 36 unique forms for *wakaes*.

6 Results and Discussion

A full paradigm for one verb is unlikely to be encountered in natural speech, or language learning contexts (Chan, 2008; Blevins and Blevins, 2009). Although the focus of this paper is not language learning, the sparsity of paradigm coverage observed in these contexts is equally relevant here. Based on various well-known corpora, Chan (2008) shows that languages with larger verbal paradigms exhibit lower coverage. Most notably, the only language with full coverage of its verbal paradigm is English, which only has six verbal forms. By contrast, Finnish has 365 verb forms and only a 40.3% saturation even though the corpus size is almost double (2.1 million words compared to the Brown corpus of 1.2 million words) that of the English counterpart.

Muradoğlu (2017) reports on the bleak data requirements to record each cell of the transitive verb in Nen. Here we have utilised the power of transformer models to leverage abstraction and statistical learning. Figure 1 shows that the model based

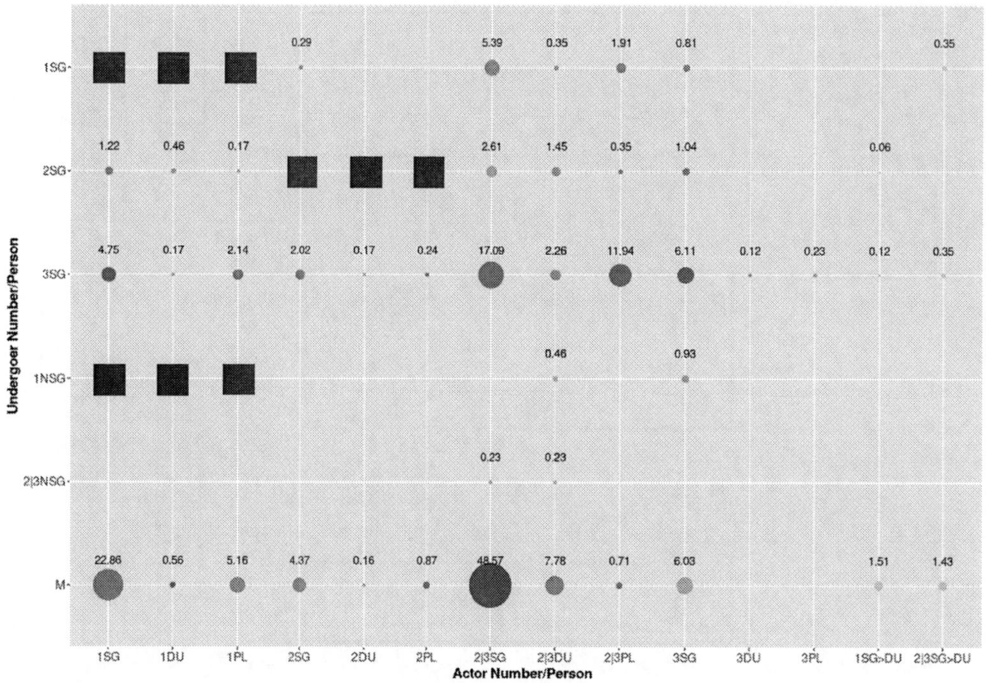

Figure 3: Relativised bubble plot of Actor and Undergoer person number for Nen. The navy blue blocks note the semantically disallowed combinations or in the case of first person acting on first person this meaning is achieved through reflexive constructions. The darker the colour (towards a purple) the more accurate the model is. Conversely the lighter the colour (lavender) the more the model struggles to produce a correct form with the corresponding features.

on the corpus does significantly better in terms of coverage. This suggests that while each combination might not be present in the corpus, the relevant information is. This typically parallels a mechanism utilised by field linguists to bootstrap the mapping of a linguistic paradigm since going through a complete paradigm for one particular verb is implausible. Instead, the circumstantial context primes language informants to showcase verbs of different semantic domains. The field linguist typically obtains part of the paradigm (either through elicitation or by natural means) for each verb. These fragments likely allow for a reconstruction of the entire paradigm. Dimensional independence allows the linguist to fill out parts of the paradigm. This task has been described as the paradigm cell filling problem (PCFC) Ackerman et al. (2009); Silfverberg and Hulden (2018); Liu and Hulden (2020).

Figure 1 shows the paradigm coverage across the four verb types in question. We contrast model-based coverage with a corpus-based account. In both instances, we follow the trajectory of one representative verb. For the model, the four test verbs are detailed in the Section 5.2.2. The corpus coverage curve follows *akingr* 'to be standing' for the positional, *owabs* 'to speak' for the middle, and *räms* 'to do/give' for the transitive verb. The model and the corpus follow *m* 'to be' since the copula verb is one entity.

The most observable behaviour shown in Figure 1 is the fluctuation across models trained across different training sizes. Although, in general, the growth is positive, we see a significant difference across each step. One explanation might be the skew within the samples added. In other words, the added examples negatively influence the generalisations built by the model. Another might be the model sensitivity to initial training data and data order. To account for the statistical variation, we report confidence bands for each verb type by measuring the variation in accuracy by dividing the test case for each verb into four random partitions. The partitions are randomly sampled as the test file is constructed in paradigmatic order. If the partitioning is performed sequentially, we might

	Corpus		Model		
	Annotation units	# of words	Training size	Annotation units	# of words
All	–	–	198,000	560,000	2,610,000
Transitive	154,000	716,000	34,000	97,000	451,000
Middle	44,000	205,000	4,000	12,000	55,000
Positional	40,000	188,000	3,000	10,000	45,000
Copula	11,000	53,000	3,000	10,000	46,000

Table 1: Extrapolated values based on the learning curve for both corpus and model-based coverage. The corpus's training size has been omitted as it does not bear any particular meaning. The numbers presented are rounded to the nearest thousand.

observe bias in one part of the paradigm, yielding large error margins.

The model shows greater coverage for the transitive, middle and copula verb types than the corpus account. Interestingly, the growth curve shows that the model-based account for positional verbs does worse than the corpus account. This is because the learning curve for the positional verb fluctuates substantially. The best-performing model for positional verbs is obtained with only 900 training examples (or 3,339 annotation units) at 16.5% coverage compared with the corpus account of *akingr* at 9% across the whole corpus. Given that the paradigm of the positional verb is the smallest among the four, we would have expected coverage to be high. A possible explanation for this might be that there are few instances of positional verbs in the corpus (26 distinct forms across seven lexemes) and, thus, the training set. We also observe looping errors as described in Shcherbakov et al. (2020), particularly for training sets below 1,000 instances.

We describe the coverage growth relative to annotation units to capture the data requirements for paradigm representation fully. The texts are segmented into annotation units to retain some of the contextual information surrounding the verb in question. These units are typically one complete sentence and most commonly correspond to a segment in ELAN (Sloetjes and Wittenburg, 2008). On average, 4.7 words per intonation unit, one of which is usually a verb. With 6,446 annotation units across the corpus, on average, for every 2.88 units, there is a distinct form encountered.

The model paradigm coverage is contrasted with that from the Nen spoken corpus. We make a point to situate the required data size for training the model (i.e., train + dev) with units that relate to the corpus to help highlight the distillation process. Typically, the model training size is measured in the number of instances. However, when collating a data set for a specific natural language processing (NLP) task – such as morphological inflection, the corpus is filtered from total words (assuming transcription exists) and later further distilled to types from tokens.

To address our third question, we analyse the frequency of the verb features along the TAM/Actor and Actor/Undergoer dimensions. We expect a strong correlation between highly frequent features in the corpus and the model accuracy for that slot. Figures 2 and 3 show the frequency of feature bundles. In both figures, the size of the bubbles corresponds to the frequency of the two sets of features in question (TAM and Actor or Actor and Undergoer). The saturation of the bubble shows how successful the model is in capturing the particular feature combination. The darker the bubble, the more likely the model will produce the correct corresponding form. These results are based on the model training with the entire training set available (2,000 instances).

As expected, both figures show a correlation between the bubble size (corpus frequency) and saturation (model accuracy). Nevertheless, there are cases where the corpus frequency is low, but the model proves to be proficient in producing the correct form. One such example is the imperfective imperative (ipfv.imp), the second person plural actor (which requires a prefix of the α series and the *-tang* suffix) makes up for 0.29% of the training data, but the model produces the correct form more than 66% of the time. One explanation might be that the rule's complexity and the chosen test verbs do not trigger allomorphic variants.

We note the morphophonological element of inflecting. While we have tried to choose regular verbs, they still exhibit a phonological layer. It is hard to disentangle such effects. One possible future direction would be to choose a list of verbs across the categories presented here which exhibit the full range of phonological phenomena observed in Nen. For example, verbs that might trigger vowel harmony and the consequent allomorphs.

We further our analysis by providing a predictive quantity of data needed to reach 100% accuracy. We utilise scipy-based (Virtanen et al., 2020) extrapolation by treating the resultant coverage curve as a learning curve. The predictions presented here are optimistic; to ensure that the predictions are based on monotonically increasing functions, we ensure that:

$$A(AU') > A(AU)$$

where A is the accuracy, AU is the annotation units and $AU' > AU$. Given the predictions' variability, the numbers are rounded to the nearest thousand. Table 1 shows that the amount of data needed for the model to reach full coverage is significantly less than a corpus-based account. In some cases, such as the transitive and middle verb, the estimated quantity is over four times less. We expect these paradigms to benefit the most from generalising as they typically display regular inflection. Additionally, the paradigm size for both is substantial.

It is tempting to draw parallels between language learning and the analysis presented here. However, we remind readers that we base our predictions on one representative verb and focus on attestation coverage rather than heuristic coverage. Furthermore, we note that heuristic coverage would require a vastly more significant quantity of data. In addition, the numbers here are for one verb only, and it does not extend to include all parts of speech.

7 Conclusion

We propose 'coverage' as a new way to measure the comprehensiveness of a corpus for morphological paradigms. Here we present this application to Nen verbal morphology. This methodology can be extended to include other parts of speech or languages.

Our results show that using deep learning approaches, more specifically the Transformer architecture (Gillioz et al., 2020; Lin et al., 2022) allows us to exploit the generalisable parts of a paradigm and thus grant us a higher coverage. The model-based account yielded higher attestation for three of the four verbs considered. In an ideal setting, each inflection feature for each word would be observed and recorded naturally. However, this is an impossible feat in real-life. Using statistics-based modelling like the Transformer model allows us to synthesise forms based on examples encountered in the training data. As a result, the existing corpus can account for more of the system than a simple count within the corpus would suggest.

We have explored the basis of the conventional wisdom of higher frequency yielding better model performance. While this holds, we observe a positive correlation between high-frequency feature combinations and model accuracy; we also see that the model can correctly generate less frequent feature combinations as well.

We provide data quantity estimations based on the learning curves generated. These predictions are meant only as a guide rather than anything definitive, as they present an optimistic case defined by the enforcement of monotonicity.

The extension of our proposed methodology to other languages with diverse morphological characteristics remains an open direction for future work.

Limitations

One major limitation of the study presented here is the microscopic tracking of one representative verb. As mentioned earlier, one potential solution is to track several verbs of each inflection type. These might be chosen based on phonological behaviour, allowing us to account for allomorphy. Another difficulty to note is the generalisability of parts of the paradigm. By using a neural approach, we wish to leverage the generalisability of the system but to cover even a subsection of language like verbal morphology fully, sometimes a direct exposure to the exceptions is needed.

Ethics Statement

Data on Nen were gathered by Evans under the projects Language and Social Cognition (ANU Aries protocol 2008/253), Languages of Southern New Guinea (ANU Aries protocol 2011/313) and The Wellsprings of Linguistic Diversity (ANU Aries Protocol 2014/224). Nen data are lodged on open access in the PARADISEC archive.

References

Farrell Ackerman, James P. Blevins, and Robert Malouf. 2009. Parts and Wholes. Implicative Patterns in Inflectional Paradigms. In *Analogy in Grammar: Form and Acquisition*, page 54–82. Oxford University Press.

Michel Jose Anzanello and Flavio Sanson Fogliatto. 2011. Learning curve models and applications: Literature review and research directions. *International Journal of Industrial Ergonomics*, 41(5):573–583.

R. Harald Baayen. 2001. *Word Frequencies*, pages 1–38. Springer Netherlands, Dordrecht, The Netherlands.

Louise Baird, Nicholas Evans, and Simon J. Greenhill. 2022. Blowing in the wind: Using 'north wind and the sun' texts to sample phoneme inventories. *Journal of the International Phonetic Association*, 52(3):453–494.

Steven Bird. 2015. Email. *Resource Network for Linguistic Diversity Discussion List.*

James P. Blevins and Juliette Blevins. 2009. *Analogy in Grammar: Form and Acquisition.* Oxford University Press.

James P. Blevins, Petar Milin, and Michael Ramscar. 2017. The zipfian paradigm cell filling problem. In *Perspectives on Morphological Organization*, pages 139 – 158. Brill, Leiden, The Netherlands.

Erwin Chan. 2008. *Structures and distributions in morphology learning*. Ph.D. thesis, University of Pennsylvania, PA,USA.

Ryan Cotterell, Christo Kirov, John Sylak-Glassman, Géraldine Walther, Ekaterina Vylomova, Patrick Xia, Manaal Faruqui, Sandra Kübler, David Yarowsky, Jason Eisner, and Mans Hulden. 2017. CoNLL-SIGMORPHON 2017 shared task: Universal morphological reinflection in 52 languages. In *Proceedings of the CoNLL SIGMORPHON 2017 Shared Task: Universal Morphological Reinflection*, pages 1–30, Vancouver. Association for Computational Linguistics.

Nicholas Evans. 2014. Positional verbs in Nen. *Oceanic Linguistics*, 53(2):225–255.

Nicholas Evans. 2015. Valency in Nen. In Andrej Malchukov and Bernard Comrie, editors, *Volume 2 Case Studies from Austronesia, the Pacific, the Americas, and Theoretical Outlook*, pages 1069–1116. De Gruyter Mouton, Berlin, München, Boston.

Nicholas Evans. 2016. Inflection in Nen. In Matthew Baerman, editor, *The Oxford Handbook of Inflection*, pages pages 543–575. Oxford University Press, USA.

Nicholas Evans. 2017. *Quantification in Nen*, pages 571–607. Springer International Publishing, Cham.

Nicholas Evans. 2019. Waiting for the Word: Distributed Deponency and the Semantic Interpretation of Number in the Nen Verb. *Morphological Perspectives. Papers In Honour of Greville G. Corbett*, pages 100–123.

Nicholas Evans. 2020. One thousand and one coconuts: Growing memories in Southern New Guinea. *The Contemporary Pacific*, 32(1):72–96.

Grant Fairbanks. 1960. *Voice and Articulation Drillbook*, Second edition. Harper & Row, New York, NY, USA.

Raphael Finkel and Gregory Stump. 2007. Principal Parts and Morphological Typology. *Morphology*, 17(1):39–75.

Anthony Gillioz, Jacky Casas, Elena Mugellini, and Omar Abou Khaled. 2020. Overview of the Transformer-based models for NLP tasks. In *2020 15th Conference on Computer Science and Information Systems (FedCSIS)*, pages 179–183.

Nikolaus P Himmelmann. 1998. Documentary and Descriptive Linguistics. *Linguistics*, 36(1):161–196.

Jordan Kodner, Salam Khalifa, Khuyagbaatar Batsuren, Hossep Dolatian, Ryan Cotterell, Faruk Akkus, Antonios Anastasopoulos, Taras Andrushko, Aryaman Arora, Nona Atanalov, Gábor Bella, Elena Budianskaya, Yustinus Ghanggo Ate, Omer Goldman, David Guriel, Simon Guriel, Silvia Guriel-Agiashvili, Witold Kieraś, Andrew Krizhanovsky, Natalia Krizhanovsky, Igor Marchenko, Magdalena Markowska, Polina Mashkovtseva, Maria Nepomniashchaya, Daria Rodionova, Karina Scheifer, Alexandra Sorova, Anastasia Yemelina, Jeremiah Young, and Ekaterina Vylomova. 2022. SIGMORPHON–UniMorph 2022 shared task 0: Generalization and typologically diverse morphological inflection. In *Proceedings of the 19th SIGMORPHON Workshop on Computational Research in Phonetics, Phonology, and Morphology*, pages 176–203, Seattle, Washington. Association for Computational Linguistics.

Tianyang Lin, Yuxin Wang, Xiangyang Liu, and Xipeng Qiu. 2022. A survey of Transformers. *AI Open*, 3:111–132.

Ling Liu and Mans Hulden. 2020. Leveraging principal parts for morphological inflection. In *Proceedings of the 17th SIGMORPHON Workshop on Computational Research in Phonetics, Phonology, and Morphology*, pages 153–161, Online. Association for Computational Linguistics.

Ling Liu and Mans Hulden. 2022. Can a Transformer pass the wug test? tuning copying bias in neural morphological inflection models. In *Proceedings of the 60th Annual Meeting of the Association for Computational Linguistics (Volume 2: Short Papers)*, pages 739–749, Dublin, Ireland. Association for Computational Linguistics.

Saliha Muradoglu, Nicholas Evans, and Hanna Suominen. 2020. To compress or not to compress? A finite-state approach to Nen verbal morphology. In *Proceedings of the 58th Annual Meeting of the Association for Computational Linguistics: Student Research Workshop*, pages 207–213, Online. Association for Computational Linguistics.

Saliha Muradoğlu. 2017. *When is enough enough ? A corpus-based study of verb inflection in a morphologically rich language (Nen).* Masters thesis, The Australian National University.

Saliha Muradoğlu, Nicholas Evans, and Ekaterina Vylomova. 2020. Modelling verbal morphology in Nen. In *Proceedings of the The 18th Annual Workshop of the Australasian Language Technology Association*, pages 43–53, Virtual Workshop. Australasian Language Technology Association.

Tiago Pimentel, Maria Ryskina, Sabrina J. Mielke, Shijie Wu, Eleanor Chodroff, Brian Leonard, Garrett Nicolai, Yustinus Ghanggo Ate, Salam Khalifa, Nizar Habash, Charbel El-Khaissi, Omer Goldman, Michael Gasser, William Lane, Matt Coler, Arturo Oncevay, Jaime Rafael Montoya Samame, Gema Celeste Silva Villegas, Adam Ek, Jean-Philippe Bernardy, Andrey Shcherbakov, Aziyana Bayyr-ool, Karina Sheifer, Sofya Ganieva, Matvey Plugaryov, Elena Klyachko, Ali Salehi, Andrew Krizhanovsky, Natalia Krizhanovsky, Clara Vania, Sardana Ivanova, Aelita Salchak, Christopher Straughn, Zoey Liu, Jonathan North Washington, Duygu Ataman, Witold Kieraś, Marcin Woliński, Totok Suhardijanto, Niklas Stoehr, Zahroh Nuriah, Shyam Ratan, Francis M. Tyers, Edoardo M. Ponti, Grant Aiton, Richard J. Hatcher, Emily Prud'hommeaux, Ritesh Kumar, Mans Hulden, Botond Barta, Dorina Lakatos, Gábor Szolnok, Judit Ács, Mohit Raj, David Yarowsky, Ryan Cotterell, Ben Ambridge, and Ekaterina Vylomova. 2021. SIGMORPHON 2021 shared task on morphological reinflection: Generalization across languages. In *Proceedings of the 18th SIGMORPHON Workshop on Computational Research in Phonetics, Phonology, and Morphology*, pages 229–259, Online. Association for Computational Linguistics.

Andrei Shcherbakov, Saliha Muradoglu, and Ekaterina Vylomova. 2020. Exploring looping effects in RNN-based architectures. In *Proceedings of the The 18th Annual Workshop of the Australasian Language Technology Association*, pages 115–120, Virtual Workshop. Australasian Language Technology Association.

Miikka Silfverberg and Mans Hulden. 2018. An encoder-decoder approach to the paradigm cell filling problem. In *Proceedings of the 2018 Conference on Empirical Methods in Natural Language Processing*, pages 2883–2889, Brussels, Belgium. Association for Computational Linguistics.

Han Sloetjes and Peter Wittenburg. 2008. Annotation by category-ELAN and ISO DCR. In *6th international Conference on Language Resources and Evaluation (LREC 2008).*

Ashish Vaswani, Noam Shazeer, Niki Parmar, Jakob Uszkoreit, Llion Jones, Aidan N Gomez, Łukasz Kaiser, and Illia Polosukhin. 2017. Attention is all you need. *Advances in Neural Information Processing Systems*, 30.

Tom Viering and Marco Loog. 2022. The Shape of Learning Curves: A Review. *IEEE Transactions on Pattern Analysis and Machine Intelligence*, pages 1–20.

Pauli Virtanen, Ralf Gommers, Travis E. Oliphant, Matt Haberland, Tyler Reddy, David Cournapeau, Evgeni Burovski, Pearu Peterson, Warren Weckesser, Jonathan Bright, Stéfan J. van der Walt, Matthew Brett, Joshua Wilson, K. Jarrod Millman, Nikolay Mayorov, Andrew R. J. Nelson, Eric Jones, Robert Kern, Eric Larson, C J Carey, İlhan Polat, Yu Feng, Eric W. Moore, Jake VanderPlas, Denis Laxalde, Josef Perktold, Robert Cimrman, Ian Henriksen, E. A. Quintero, Charles R. Harris, Anne M. Archibald, Antônio H. Ribeiro, Fabian Pedregosa, Paul van Mulbregt, and SciPy 1.0 Contributors. 2020. SciPy 1.0: Fundamental Algorithms for Scientific Computing in Python. *Nature Methods*, 17:261–272.

Shijie Wu, Ryan Cotterell, and Mans Hulden. 2021. Applying the transformer to character-level transduction. In *Proceedings of the 16th Conference of the European Chapter of the Association for Computational Linguistics: Main Volume*, pages 1901–1907, Online. Association for Computational Linguistics.

A Appendix: Inflection categories

IPFV.FIMP:	Future Imperfective
IPFV.IMP:	Imperfective Imperative
IPFV.MIMP:	Mediated imperative
IPFV.NPHD:	Imperfective Nonprehodiernal
IPFV.YPST:	Imperfective Yesterday Past
IPFV.RMPST:	Imperfective Remote Past
NEUT.PRIM:	Neutral Primordial
NEUT.PRET:	Neutral Preterite
NEUT.PIRR:	Neutral Irrealis
PFV.IMP:	Perfective Imperative
PFV.FUT:	Perfective Future
PFV.PST:	Perfective Past

Multilingual Automatic Extraction of Linguistic Data from Grammars

Albert Kornilov
National Research University
Higher School of Economics
Moscow, Russia
albert.kornilov801@gmail.com

Abstract

One of the goals of field linguistics is compilation of descriptive grammars for relatively little-studied languages. Until recently, extracting linguistic characteristics from grammatical descriptions and creating databases based on them was done manually. The aim of this paper is to apply methods of multilingual automatic information extraction to grammatical descriptions written in different languages of the world: we present a search engine for grammars, which would accelerate the tedious and time-consuming process of searching for information about linguistic features and facilitate research in the field of linguistic typology.

1 Introduction

This work is dedicated to methods of information extraction, one of the subtasks of natural language processing. Methods of information extraction are widely used to create search engines. In addition to web services designed to search for internet websites that are relevant to the user's request, there is a need for highly specialized search engines for scientific publications, including linguistic ones.

One of the publication types in field linguistics is a descriptive grammar, which is a description of phonetic, morphological, syntactic, semantic and other characteristics of a particular language. Until recently, extracting language characteristics from descriptive grammars and creating databases based on them was done manually. For instance, The World Atlas of Language Structures[1], originally published as a book (Haspelmath et al., 2005), contains information on 144 characteristics for over 2600 languages.

Searching for information about a multitude of features is a long and labor-intensive process, albeit a portion of grammars is available not only in paper form, but also in digitized form: grammars from different time periods (from missionary grammars to modern papers) created by researchers from different countries do not have a single structure. Furthermore, a simple search for a word in a document can return dozens of occurrences, and not all of them will be relevant to the query.

The purpose of this work is to create a search engine for grammars, which would facilitate and speed up the process of finding information about language characteristics. The paper considers two methods of information extraction (BM25 and a reranking model based on BERT). The materials for the demonstration of the search engine include grammars presented on Google Drive[2].

Section 2 will analyze the already existing works pertaining to the task of automatic extraction of data from grammars; in Section 3, the methods used for data preprocessing will be described. Section 4 will discuss the two methods used for information extraction. In Section 5, we will compare the results obtained using the two methods and demonstrate the features of the search engine web application.

2 Review of Existing Approaches

At the moment, the subject of automatic information extraction of data from grammars is relatively little-studied. Several scientific papers regarding the methodology for extracting information from grammars using frame semantic parsers have been published by members of Språkbanken, a research and development unit at the University of Gothenburg, Sweden: (Virk et al., 2017; Virk et al., 2019; Virk et al., 2020; Virk et al., 2021). The methodology proposed by Språkbanken is illustrated in (Virk et al., 2019) using the following hypothetical sentence from a grammar as an example:

> The adjectives follow the noun they qualify.

[1] https://wals.info/

[2] https://drive.google.com/drive/folders/1FUunY_30HCKUsSixwczsxRaJ71fAb9Ii

Proceedings of the Second Workshop on NLP Applications to Field Linguistics, pages 86–94
May 6, 2023 ©2023 Association for Computational Linguistics

An answer to the following question: "What is the order of adjectives and nouns in the language?" is to be chosen from the values "noun-adjective", "adjective-noun", and "both". Based on the labels assigned to the predicate "follow", the subject "adjectives", and the object "noun" by the semantic parser, the option "noun-adjective" is selected as an answer to the question and entered into the database.

Semantic parsers based on tagged text corpora are usually not sufficient to describe semantic frames found in grammars. (Virk et al., 2020) describes the functionality of a highly specialized semantic parser for linguistic publications, created on the basis of LingFN. LingFN is a corpus of grammars in English with annotated semantic frames, described in in (Malm et al., 2018). Extracting information from grammars written in languages other than English would require creating highly specialized parsers for each of the languages. Since a single specialized parser is not a multilingual solution, further this paper will discuss methods that are not based on frame semantics.

A simpler method is used in (Hammarström et al., 2020): to find out if a certain phenomenon is present in the language, the frequency of the corresponding term in the text of the grammar is counted. Occurrences of a term in the context of negative polarity items ("in language X [there is no phenomenon Y] | [missing category Y] | [category Y not found]") are excluded. Based on the distribution of occurrences of each term in grammars, a frequency threshold is calculated. Only terms with a frequency above the threshold are categories potentially present in the language. This method does not require significant time spent on annotating corpora and is universal for grammars written in any language, which greatly facilitates automatic creation of databases of linguistic characteristics.

However, the methods described in (Virk et al., 2017; Virk et al., 2019; Virk et al., 2020; Virk et al., 2021; Hammarström et al., 2020) are effective for building language databases in the form of tables, where at the intersection of a row with the name of the language and the column with the name of the category is an answer to a question (for example, "noun-adjective") or a truth value indicating presence or absence of a particular category in the language.

The table format does not fully meet the goals of our work, since it is not enough for a search engine to extract a single truth value; it is more crucial to extract a paragraph which describes the specific features of the desired language characteristic, together with the glosses and examples. Therefore, it has been decided to use methods that rank documents (paragraphs) according to their relevance to the search query entered by the user in order to return the original paragraph from the grammar in response to the query. The chosen approach does not perform any final feature extraction, but leaves the ultimate decision to the linguist.

3 Data

The grammars from which the search engine application extracts information are presented on Google Drive in the Grammars folder. The source code of the application is available on[3].

Each grammar is presented in a .pdf file. The table grammars_database.xslx (stored in the source code repository) contains meta-information for each grammar: the full path to the file, availability of an OCR layer ("Searchable"/"Not searchable"), the language described in the grammar, and the language the grammar is in. Initially, some files did not have an OCR layer. Such files were processed using the ocrmypdf[4] library.

For the subsequent information extraction, the contents of each file were preprocessed. The grammars were parsed using the pdftotext[5] library and divided into paragraphs. A combination of two spaces was taken as a separator. After separation, extra spaces were removed from the beginning and end of each paragraph. Since there are frequent cases of a paragraph being split between two pages, after separation, each pair of adjacent paragraphs was checked: if the second paragraph does not start with a capital letter and/or the first one does not end with a dot, ellipsis, question mark or exclamation mark, then they were connected again into a single paragraph.

Further, each paragraph was divided into tokens using the spaCy[6] library. spaCy was chosen because it currently implements text preprocessing methods for 22 languages. The paragraphs underwent tokenization; punctuation marks, numbers, and stop words were removed. The lists of tokens and their corresponding page numbers were saved

[3]https://github.com/grammars-data-extraction/linguistic_data_extraction

[4]https://github.com/ocrmypdf/OCRmyPDF

[5]https://pypi.org/project/pdftotext/

[6]https://spacy.io/

in .json files in the Grammars_Page_Numbers folder in the repository in order that the search algorithm would work with preprocessed data and not with the original .pdf file.

After the tokenization, the paragraphs were lemmatized, and the lists of lemmas were saved as .json files in the Grammars_Lemmas folder.

4 Methods for Ranking Paragraphs by Relevance to the Query

After the data has been divided into paragraphs and preprocessed, the search engine itself was implemented. It accepts a query from the user, determines which of the paragraphs are relevant to the query, and returns them. To calculate relevance, this paper uses the BM25 algorithm and a combination of BM25 with BERT embeddings.

4.1 BM25

BM25 is a family of functions that assign a relevance score to the search query to each of the documents (in our case, each of the paragraphs). The paper uses the function described in (Trotman et al., 2012) and implemented in the BM25Okapi class of the rank-bm25[7] library:

$$BM25(Q, d) =$$

$$= \sum_{t \in Q}^{n} IDF(t) \frac{(k_i + 1) \cdot tf_{td}}{tf_{td} + k_1 \cdot (1 - b + b \cdot \frac{L_d}{L_{avg}})}$$

$$IDF(t) = log \frac{N - df_t + 0.5}{df_t + 0.5}$$

Q: the query entered by the user;

d: the paragraph for which the relevance is determined;

tf_{td}: the number of occurrences of the token in the paragraph;

df_t: the number of paragraphs in the grammar that contain the token;

N: the total number of paragraphs in the grammar;

L_d: the number of tokens in the paragraph;

L_{avg}: the mean of the number of tokens for all paragraphs.

4.2 BERT

Among many other NLP tasks, BERT can be used to rank documents by relevance to a query: it assigns a vector to the query and to each paragraph from the document. The more relevant the query and the paragraph are to each other, the greater the cosine similarity is between them. For this paper, the bert-base-multilingual-cased model[8] was used, which supports 104 languages.

Since creating sentence embeddings using BERT and calculating the cosine similarity for each paragraph has a greater algorithmic complexity than BM25, in order to optimize the running time a decision was made to use the combined BM25 + BERT reranking method, decribed in (Nogueira and Cho, 2019).

4.3 BM25 + BERT Reranking

The combined method is structured as follows: using a simpler ranking method (in our case, BM25), n paragraphs relevant to the query are selected from the document, and afterwards k paragraphs ($k < n$) are selected from them using a more algorithmically complex method (in our case, the BERT embedder). When developing a search engine for grammars, it was decided to use only BM25 and the combined method, refraining from using BERT without BM25, since a search engine, unlike algorithms used for creating databases, works in real time, and significant time delays after the user enters a query are unacceptable.

5 A Solution to the Problem of Multilinguality

Since the goal of this paper is to create a search engine that is not exclusive to grammars written in English, it is necessary to implement an algorithm for automatically translating the user's query from English into other languages. Google Translate and libraries based on it are not suitable for this task: results for translating linguistic terms into other languages are in most cases incorrect. For instance, the term "reduplication" is translated from English into German as "Verdoppelung" ("doubling"), not "Reduplikation".

Consequently, it was decided to use another method of translating linguistic terms into different languages: using Wikipedia.

The HTML code of the Wikipedia page called "Reduplication" in English contains links to pages about the same term in other languages. The method for extracting page titles in the desired language was implemented using the beautiful-

[7] https://github.com/dorianbrown/rank_bm25

[8] https://huggingface.co/bert-base-multilingual-cased

soup4[9] library. In addition to titles of articles, it was decided to extract their summaries using the Wikipedia[10] library. Example: summary for the term "Ergative case"[11] in English (accessed 23 Feb. 2023):

> In grammar, the ergative case (abbreviated ERG) is the grammatical case that identifies a nominal phrase as the agent of a transitive verb in ergative–absolutive languages.

Using a summary as a query increases the likelihood of extracting a relevant paragraph from the grammar, as it may contain words, linguistic terms, and abbreviations that are often found in the context of the term requested by the user: for instance, the summary for the Wikipedia article "Ergative case" contains the abbreviation "ERG" and related terms "agent", "transitive verb", and "absolutive".

Each summary is extracted from Wikipedia, tokenized, and lemmatized only once. The summaries themselves and the lists of tokens corresponding to them are saved in .json files in the Grammars_Summaries folder in the repository.

6 Results

6.1 The Functionality of the Search Engine

In this section, the functionality of the search engine will be demonstrated on the example of the query "Plural" and a grammar of the Angami language (McCabe, 1887). The BM25 algorithm returns the five most relevant paragraphs from the grammar; in the combined algorithm, BM25 selects ten paragraphs and afterwards BERT selects the five most relevant ones out of them. The extracted paragraphs are shown in Table 1. In this particular case, the set of paragraphs selected by the two methods is the same; however, the paragraph containing the information about the most common method for expressing the singular and the plural in Angami (lack of marking) was placed higher by BM25 than by the combined method.

The interface of the search engine application is presented in Figure 1. The user is prompted to select an algorithm from the top menu and enter the name of the language and the desired linguistic feature. The application returns the five most relevant paragraphs from each grammar describing the language. After every paragraph, its source pages from the file with the grammar are displayed, in order for the user to be able to instantly see the relevant context and glosses with examples. The repository stores only a part of the grammars; the remaining grammars are copied from the Google Drive using the rclone[12] script upon being requested by the user.

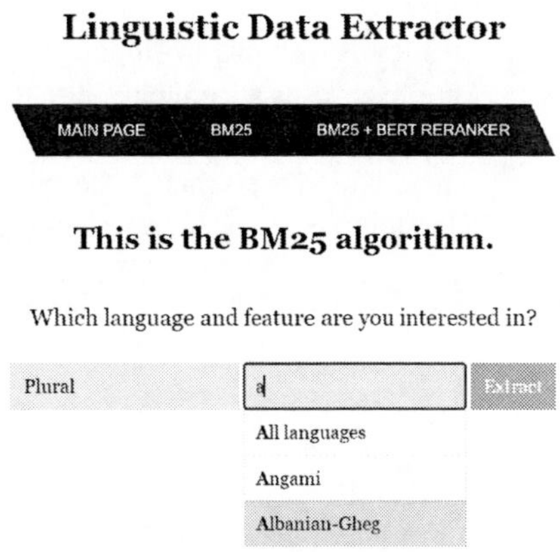

Figure 1: The web interface of the search engine.

The features currently available in the demo version of the search engine are the following: Reduplication, Plural, Declension, Nominative case, Ergative case, Absolutive case, Accusative case, Word order. Any feature with its own page on Wikipedia can potentially be integrated into the functionality of the application.

The demo version supports extraction of characteristics of the following languages: Samaritan Aramaic, Lule, Angami, Javanese, Sangir, Pampangan, Hawaiian, Albanian-Gheg, Karelian, Tibetan. Since for typological research entering the language name should be non-mandatory, an additional option "All languages" has been added to the interface.

6.2 A Qualitative Evaluation

The search engine has been tested on over 500 grammars written in some of the most spoken European languages (English, German, French, Spanish, Italian, Russian, Dutch). The testing procedure included extracting information on each of the linguistic features available in the demo version from each of the grammars.

While a quantitative evaluation of the search engine (e. g. calculation of metrics) is difficult to

[9] https://pypi.org/project/beautifulsoup4/

[10] https://pypi.org/project/wikipedia/

[11] https://en.wikipedia.org/wiki/Ergative_case

[12] https://rclone.org

Rank	BM25	BM25 + BERT Reranking
1	In these examples no inflections nor descriptive words are em ployed to denote the singular or plural.	The plural is the same as the third person plural of the personal pronoun Hāko these.
2	The plural is the same as the third person plural of the personal pronoun Hāko these.	As a general rule , however, when it is desired to clearly mark the singular and plural, the numeral adjective po = " one," is used to denote the singular, and the suffix ko the plural : I saw a dog in your house . Ā unki nu tefüh po ngulé.
3	As a general rule , however, when it is desired to clearly mark the singular and plural, the numeral adjective po = " one," is used to denote the singular, and the suffix ko the plural : I saw a dog in your house . Ā unki nu tefüh po ngulé.	In these examples no inflections nor descriptive words are em ployed to denote the singular or plural.
4	The reflexive pronoun " self," " myself," " himself, " &c. , is ren dered by the word the or tha . It is not declined, and has but one form for the singular and plural I came myself = A the vorwe.	The reflexive pronoun " self," " myself," " himself, " &c. , is ren dered by the word the or tha . It is not declined, and has but one form for the singular and plural I came myself = A the vorwe.
5	This section treats of nouns under the heads "Gender," " Number " and " Case." I.-GENDER .	This section treats of nouns under the heads "Gender," " Number " and " Case." I.-GENDER .

Table 1: Comparison of BM25 and BM25 + BERT Reranking on the example of the query "Plural" and the grammar (McCabe, 1887).

conduct due to the fact that final feature extraction is not performed, the empirical results show the following:

(i) Readability of outputs with glosses leaves room for improvement. This problem is mitigated by outputting the source pages from the file with the grammar. An example of an output with glosses and the corresponding fragment of the source page are given in Figure 2 and Figure 3 in Appendix A respectively.

(ii) It is not the case that division of grammars into paragraphs is optimal for all descriptive grammars, since they lack common structure: paragraphs that are overly long (containing large blocks of glosses and examples) or overly short (containing only one of the terms from the query) occasionally occur among the results. Outputting the source pages partially mitigates this problem as well, since the majority of the overly short paragraphs are titles of sections and subsections in the descriptive grammars. An example of an overly long output is given in Figure 4, and an example of an overly short output with its source page fragment is presented in Figure 5 in Appendix A.

6.3 Coverage of Linguistic Features in Wikipedia

In order to provide a quantitative evaluation of Wikipedia as the basis of the search engine, we took the list of linguistic features from The World Atlas of Language Structures[13] and manually annotated their corresponding Wikipedia entries. The titles of the entries were translated into German, French, Spanish, Italian, Russian, and Dutch using the Wikipedia[14] library. Statistics on the coverage of the linguistic features in Wikipedia articles have been calculated for all seven languages. The result of the evaluation is given in Table 2, and the table with the annotations (Coverage_of_linguistic_phenomena_in_Wikipedia.xlsx) is available in the source code repository.

Table 2 shows that 34 features out of 192 have their own Wikipedia entries in the English language. Several features are expressed by a com-

[13]https://wals.info/

[14]https://pypi.org/project/wikipedia/

Coverage	Yes	Partially	No
German	22	131	39
French	18	124	50
Spanish	17	137	38
Italian	19	91	82
Russian	18	131	53
Dutch	14	127	51
Average	**18**	**123.5**	**52.2**
English	**34**	**143**	**15**

Table 2: Coverage of linguistic features in Wikipedia articles (accessed 30 March 2023).

bination of Wikipedia entries instead of a single one. For instance, feature 52A, Comitatives and Instrumentals, is covered by three entries: Comitative case, Instrumental case, and Instrumental-comitative case. The average number of features marked with "Yes" for the other six languages is 18 (only 52.9% of the corresponding number for English), while the average number of missing features for the six languages is 348% of the number of missing features in the English Wikipedia.

Since the search engine outputs paragraphs and leaves the final decision to the linguist, the limitations on queries are less strict than for models intended for final feature extraction. Consequently, we introduce the third category, "Partially", in order to mitigate the imbalance: the linguistic features belonging to it are more specific than the corresponding articles. For example, feature 36A, The Associative Plural, has no matching article in the English Wikipedia and therefore corresponds to the article with the title "Plural".

The advantage of using Wikipedia is coverage of linguistic features that are not present in WALS: for instance, Assimilation, Aorist, Semelfactive, Mass noun, Cardinal numeral, and Vowel harmony.

7 Conclusion

This paper presents a search engine web application that allows automatic extraction of information from grammars written in different languages of the world. Two information extraction methods (classical BM25 and the combined method based on BM25 + reranking with BERT) have been compared to each other regarding the task of extracting linguistic information relevant to the user's query. The search algorithm has been integrated with Wikipedia.

The implemented system makes it possible to get an impression of the total complexity of the task of automatic information extraction from scientific publications and opens up the possibility for massive automated research in the field of linguistic typology, facilitating the routine task of extracting information from grammatical descriptions and allowing researchers to direct the time to solving problems that require advanced expertise.

Limitations

The work presented in the paper has potential limitations. To begin with, particular attention should be paid to normalization of terminology, which varies in grammatical descriptions belonging to different scientific schools and eras. Furthermore, the multilinguality of the system requires further development: testing of the search engine was only carried out for grammars written in some of the most spoken European languages, due to grammars in other languages being accessible in significantly smaller quantities. Moreover, the performance of the search engine can potentially be improved by using a faster system (for instance, S3) rather than accessing the Google Drive storage through rclone. In addition, while using Wikipedia is a potential solution to the problem of multilinguality, it is a user-generated source, and using it may potentially yield unexpected or unreliable results. Ultimately, the graphical interface can be supplemented with tools for collecting and analyzing user feedback. To further improve user experience, it is planned to carry out further testing of the system on experts conducting research in the field of linguistic typology.

Ethics Statement

The dataset originally used for testing the search engine partially consisted of grammars subject to copyright. In order to avoid any form of copyright infringement, we left only ten grammars in Google Drive and in the source code repository. The grammars are stored in the dataset solely for the purpose of demonstrating the functionality of the search engine. Each of the ten grammars is part of the open-access set maintained by Språkbanken[15], is at least 100 years old, and is not subject to copyright.

[15] https://spraakbanken.gu.se/blogg/index.php/2020/04/07/a-multilingual-annotated-corpus-of-worlds-natural-language-descriptions/

Acknowledgements

First and foremost, we would like to express our gratitude to Oleg Serikov (National Research University Higher School of Economics, AIRI, MIPT, RAS Linguistics) for his continuous support and guidance throughout the entire process of creating the search engine. In addition, we are grateful to the anonymous reviewers for their suggestions, which substantially improved this paper. Moreover, we would like to extend our thanks to Mason Gilliam (University of Texas at Austin) for valuable insights regarding information retrieval algorithms.

References

Antonio Machoni de Cerdeña. 1877. *Arte y vocabulario de la lengua lule y tonocoté...* Reimpreso por Pablo E. Coni.

Harald Hammarström, One-Soon Her, and Marc Allassonnière-Tang. 2020. Term spotting: A quick-and-dirty method for extracting typological features of language from grammatical descriptions. In *Selected contributions from the Eighth Swedish Language Technology Conference (SLTC-2020)*, pages 27–34.

Martin Haspelmath, Matthew S Dryer, David Gil, and Bernard Comrie. 2005. *The world atlas of language structures*. OUP Oxford.

Itziar Laka. 1996. *A brief grammar of Euskara, the Basque language*. Univ. of the Basque Country.

Per Malm, Shafqat Mumtaz Virk, Lars Borin, and Anju Saxena. 2018. Lingfn: Towards a framenet for the linguistics domain. In *11th edition of the Language Resources and Evaluation Conference, 7-12 May 2018, Miyazaki (Japan)*, pages 37–43.

Robert Blair McCabe. 1887. *Outline Grammar of the Angāmi Nāgā Language: With a Vocabulary and Illustrative Sentences*. Superintendent of Government Printing.

Rodrigo Nogueira and Kyunghyun Cho. 2019. Passage re-ranking with bert. *arXiv preprint arXiv:1901.04085*.

Andrew Trotman, Xiangfei Jia, and Matt Crane. 2012. Towards an efficient and effective search engine. In *OSIR@ SIGIR*, pages 40–47.

Shafqat Mumtaz Virk, Lars Borin, Anju Saxena, and Harald Hammarström. 2017. Automatic extraction of typological linguistic features from descriptive grammars. In *Text, Speech, and Dialogue: 20th International Conference, TSD 2017, Prague, Czech Republic, August 27-31, 2017, Proceedings 20*, pages 111–119. Springer.

Shafqat Mumtaz Virk, Daniel Foster, Azam Sheikh Muhammad, and Raheela Saleem. 2021. A deep learning system for automatic extraction of typological linguistic information from descriptive grammars. In *Proceedings of the International Conference on Recent Advances in Natural Language Processing (RANLP 2021)*, pages 1480–1489.

Shafqat Mumtaz Virk, Harald Hammarström, Lars Borin, Markus Forsberg, SK Wichmann, Maxim Ionov, John P McCrae, Christian Chiarcos, Thierry Declerck, Julia Bosque-Gil, et al. 2020. From linguistic descriptions to language profiles. In *Proceedings of the 7th Workshop on Linked Data in Linguistics (LDL-2020)*, pages 23–27.

Shafqat Mumtaz Virk, Azam Sheikh Muhammad, Lars Borin, Muhammad Irfan Aslam, Saania Iqbal, and Nazia Khurram. 2019. Exploiting frame-semantics and frame-semantic parsing for automatic extraction of typological information from descriptive grammars of natural languages. In *Proceedings of the International Conference on Recent Advances in Natural Language Processing (RANLP 2019)*, pages 1247–1256.

Michael Weiers. 2013. *Die Sprache der Moghol der Provinz Herat in Afghanistan: Sprachmaterial, Grammatik, Wortliste*, volume 49. Springer-Verlag.

A Output Examples

Figure 2, Figure 3, Figure 4, and Figure 5 show examples of outputs of the search engine.

Grammars/Other/Basque Language, A Brief Grammar of Euskara (Laka).pdf
Result №3.

Noun phrases are inflected for ergative case if they are subjects of transitive verbs:
(5)
a. zazpi gizonek ekarri dute pianoa
seven man-E brought have piano-det
'seven men have brought the piano'
b. etxeko txakurrak ikusi gaitu
house-of dog-det-E seen us-has
'the dog of the house has seen us'
c. Mirenen anaiek ez dakite kanta hau
Miren-gen brother-detpl-E not know song this
'Miren's brothers don't know this song'

Figure 2: An example of an output with glosses. Query: Ergative case. Method: BM-25. Language: Basque. Descriptive grammar: (Laka, 1996).

(5)

a. zazpi gizonek ekarri dute pianoa
seven man-E brought have piano-det
'seven men have brought the piano'

b. etxeko txakurrak ikusi gaitu
house-of dog-det-E seen us-has
'the dog of the house has seen us'

c. Mirenen anaiek ez dakite kanta hau
Miren-gen brother-det_{pl}-E not know song this
'Miren's brothers don't know this song'

(5a) illustrates our previous example Noun phrase as the subject of the transitive verb **ekarri** 'to bring'. (5b) illustrates a singular definite Noun phrase marked with ergative case, since it is the subject of the verb **ikusi** 'to see'. Finally, (5c) illustrates a plural definite Noun phrase inflected for ergative. Note that when the ergative marker **k** attaches to the plural determiner **ak**, the resulting form is **ek**. Again, this Noun phrase is the subject of a transitive verb, in this case, **jakin** 'to know'. Along these lines, it must also be noted that the combination of the proximity determiner **ok** and ergative **k** yields **ok**. Thus, regarding Noun phrases ending in the proximity dterminer **ok**, the absolutive and the nominative forms are identical; this is called 'syncretism'.

Figure 3: A fragment of a source page with glosses from a file with a grammar. Query: Ergative case. Method: BM-25. Language: Basque. Descriptive grammar: (Laka, 1996).

Grammars/Mongolic/Moghol, Die Sprache der (Weiers).pdf
Result №3.

Morphologie 113
B. Nomina
1. Pluralbildung 1
Die Moghol-Sprache besitzt die Pluralsuffixe -df-t, -nud und -s. Vielfach wird trotz eines verwendeten Pluralsuffixes nur die Einzahl zum Ausdruck gebracht. Um anzuzeigen, wann dies der Fall ist, wollen wir zwei Kategorien unterscheiden: 1. Die grammatisch-formale: Singular (S) und Plural (P). 2. Die semantische: Einzahl (E) und Mehrzahl (M). Hieraus ergeben sich hinsichtlich der Pluralbezeichnung durch Suffixe die Kombinationen EP und MP. Bei Mehrzahlwortern haben wir die Kombination MS. Die semantische Kategorie bezeichnen wir bei den Kombinationen immer als die erste. Die Kombination EP hat oftmals Kollektivbedeutung, worunter wir entweder die Bezeichnung einer Gesamtheit, z. B. "der Mensch" im Sinne der gesamten Menschheit, oder einer Gesamtgruppe verstehen, z.B. "Hirse" als Gesamtgruppe innerhalb verschiedener Getreidesorten. Als Belege fiihren wir nachstehend meist nur Einzelworter und deren Funktion an, da das Gesamtbeispiel ohne Schwierigkeiten in den Sprachmaterialien aufzufinden ist.
1. -df-t
Das weitaus haufigste Suffix -d steht iiberwiegend im Nominativ PI. von vokalisch auslautenden und n-Stammen, deren n beim Suffixantritt abfallt. -t steht nach den gleichen Stammen, jedoch meist in einem der obliquen Kasus oder vor enklitischen Personalpronomina, kurz als Silbenbeginn vor einem folgenden, oft akzentuierten Vokai. Das Suffix bezieht

Figure 4: An example of an overly long output. Query: Plural. Method: BM-25. Language: Moghol. Descriptive grammar: (Weiers, 2013).

Grammars/Arte y vocabulario de la lengua lule o tonocoté.pdf
Result №5.

44ARTE DE LA LENGUA
5. Pongo por ejemplo :
Nominativo ... Pelé ....

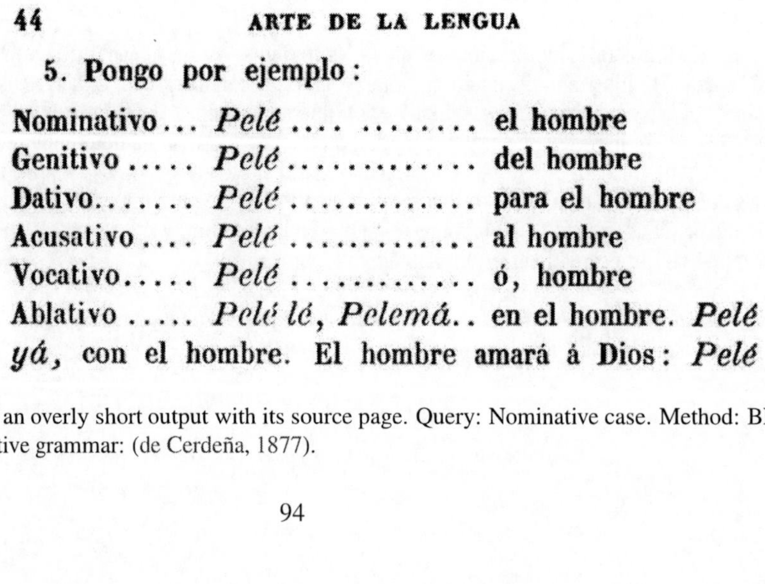
44 ARTE DE LA LENGUA

5. Pongo por ejemplo:

Nominativo... *Pelé* .... el hombre
Genitivo ..... *Pelé* .... del hombre
Dativo....... *Pelé* .... para el hombre
Acusativo .... *Pelé* .... al hombre
Vocativo..... *Pelé* .... ó, hombre
Ablativo ..... *Pelé lé, Pelemá*.. en el hombre. *Pelé yá*, con el hombre. El hombre amará á Dios: *Pelé*

Figure 5: An example of an overly short output with its source page. Query: Nominative case. Method: BM-25. Language: Lule. Descriptive grammar: (de Cerdeña, 1877).

Author Index

Association for Computational Linguistics
209 N. Eighth Street
Stroudsburg, Pennsylvania 18360

ISBN 978-1-7138-9050-8

9 781713 890508

CURRAN ASSOCIATES INC.
proceedings.com